The Whaling Trade of North-East England 1750-1850

Tony Barrow

University of Sunderland Press

ISBN 1 87 37 57 83-2

First published 2001

Cover Design by Tim Murphy Creative Solutions

Published in Great Britain by
The University of Sunderland Press
in association with Business Education Publishers Limited
The Solar Building
Doxford International
Sunderland
SR3 3XW

Tel: 0191 5252410
Fax: 0191 5201815

British Cataloguing-in-Publications Data
A catalogue record for this book is available from the British Library

Printed in Great Britain by Athenaeum Press Limited

For Tim and Flo

Contents

Contents

Tables

Illustrations

Cover

Part One Inserts

Part Two Inserts

Abbreviations

BPP	British Parliamentary Papers
DRO	Durham County Record Office
HTH	Hull Trinity House
NMM	National Maritime Museum
NRO	Northumberland Record Office
NSLS	North Shields Local Studies Library
PRO	Public Record Office
SRO	Scottish Record Office
TWAD	Tyne Wear Archives Department
WLPS	Whitby Literary and Philosophical Society

Preface

This book originated more than ten years ago as part of my Ph.D thesis. Since then the demands of a young family, of further research and a full time job, have delayed its completion. But delay can be a constructive as well as frustrating experience. It provides opportunities for reflection and time to discover new sources of information. Delay also facilitates the development of new connections and the consolidation of older ones. Numerous individuals have lent their support and encouragement to this project over the years.

I was originally drawn to the Whale Fishery of north-east England by a short list of primary sources compiled by Roger Sims who was then at Tyne Wear Archives Department. I soon discovered that the late Tom Marshall, local studies librarian at Gateshead Central Library, had already indexed almost all of the references to whales and whaling in local newspaper collections long before I happened upon the subject. I am grateful to Roger and Tom for providing the original stimulus to my research. Particular thanks are also due to Arthur Credland, Keeper of the Town Docks Museum at Hull and Adrian Osler, formerly curator of Maritime Collections at Tyne Wear Museums, for their unstinting advice and encouragement over many years. Dr. David Rowe, my principal Ph.D supervisor and Professor Norman McCord, taught me how to write history in the first place, whilst countless others have helped to sustain my research. The consistent support of my colleagues in the History Department at Newcastle College, Mike Furlonger and Dr. Elizabeth O'Donnell has been much appreciated though, perhaps, infrequently expressed. Similarly, the willingness of local historians, genealogists and fellow travellers in the field of maritime history, to correspond and share information has been an enriching experience. In particular, a mention in dispatches is due to: Dr. David J. Starkey, Dr. Stephen Fisher, Dick Keyes, Dave Bond, Dr. Robb Robinson, Professor John Armstrong, John Gaskin, Francis Cowe, Peter Barton, Tony Northway, Jim Troup, Nick Redman, Moira Ruddick, Linda Bankier, Eileen Carnaffin, Dr. W. Gillies-Ross, Dave Ridley, Tony Pawlyn and Dr. Stuart Frank, curator of the Kendall Whaling Museum, Sharon, Massachusetts.

The project has also benefited, periodically, from some generous financial support. A grant from The Twenty Seven Foundation, Institute of Historical Research in

1991, facilitated research of material contained within the Robertson Archive at Stromness in Orkney. Further support from The Historical Association and Dr. Anthea Bushby of Hexham has contributed to subsidise some of the publication costs and enabled the inclusion of illustrations that have undoubtedly enhanced the quality of the finished product. Thanks are also due to the descendants of some old whaling families who allowed access to artefacts and heirlooms. In particular, I wish to acknowledge the contributions of Penelope and the late Christopher Bray who allowed me regular and unrestricted use of The George Palmer Collection and my family the use of 'Claridges' for some memorable Southwold summers. Mr. Maurice Williamson of Bircham Toft near Kings Lynn, for permission to use the Journal of Dr. James Williamson (1814-1899) surgeon of *Lady Jane.* John Milward of Windsor gave permission to copy and use a unique photograph–that of Captain John Patterson (1805-1879) of North Shields–last of the old whaler captains of north-east England. Thanks are also due to the staff of the Local Studies Department, Newcastle Central Library, Tyne Wear Archives Department, Northumberland Record Office, Newcastle Literary and Philosophical Society, Scottish Record Office, Professor Donald Woodward, Hon. Archivist to the Master and Brethren of Hull Trinity House and Whitby Literary and Philosophical Society. As with so many other projects in the past, the ability to call upon the professional skills and photographic expertise of Stuart Wilkin of Newcastle College has been invaluable.

Naturally, I also wish to acknowledge the individual contributions of various members of my family. My wife Val, secretary, research assistant, counsellor and homemaker who has always provided a supportive environment in which to write. My daughters, Ailsa, Harriet, Emma and Amy who have all lived through my obsession with whales and whaling for as long as they can remember. For them the end is in sight!! Finally, a special mention is due to my sister, Pat Barrow, who has shared the burdens of this book ever since I decided to write it. It is her book and her achievement as much as it is mine. All of the technical aspects of the text and its layout, maps, tables and appendices are her work. A combination of patience, tenacity, cheerfulness and resilience enabled her to transform the chaos of countless revisions and amendments into a coherent and attractive book. She is bound to breathe an enormous sigh of relief and enjoy a personal sense of satisfaction in a job well done. As a joint effort the book is dedicated to our parents who laid the foundations of successful careers and never failed to provide consistent support. The only disappointment of delay has been that Dad, Tim Barrow, did not live to see it completed.

Tony Barrow
October 2000

Brief biography of the author

Tony Barrow is Lecturer in History and Archaeology at Newcastle College where he has worked for more than twenty years. He studied at Newcastle University and obtained his Ph.D from Newcastle Polytechnic as it then was, in 1989, for research into The North East Coast Whaling Trade 1750-1850. As a member of the International Society for Nautical Research and a committee member of the British Commission for Maritime History he is widely consulted for his knowledge of regional ships and shipping in the age of sail, and is the author of numerous articles about the maritime history of the region. His other books include; *Tall Ships:Two Rivers* (with A.Osler); *Press Gangs and Privateers: Aspects of the Maritime History of North East England; Walks around the Old Coal Ports of Northumberland* and its companion volume *Walks around the Old Grain Ports of Northumberland.*

The Whaling Trade of North-East England 1750-1850

Tony Barrow

Introduction

More than one hundred and fifty years ago, in June 1849, *Lady Jane*, last of the old sailing whalers of north-east England was wrecked in the Canadian Arctic. She was one of a number of ships overwhelmed by a mass of floating ice in Melville Bay, a notorious graveyard of stout old whaleships. Captain Patterson and his crew of 50 men lowered the whaleboats onto the ice and saved what they could of their clothes and provisions. They camped on the ice for four days in the hope that the remaining ship, a New England whaler called *McLellan*, would survive her own ordeal with the pack ice. When it looked to be impossible that the *McLellan* would survive, Patterson made a vital decision. He divided provisions amongst the crew of *Lady Jane* and at seven o'clock in the evening launched the whaleboats into the sea. It was bitterly cold and the wind blew fresh from the north-east. In the perpetual twilight of an Arctic night the little flotilla sailed along the edge of the pack ice. Wherever the route was obstructed, the Greenlandmen pulled their whaleboats from the sea and dragged them across icefields, or around grounded icebergs, until they regained open water. They reached land the following morning. After a brief stop for food and rest they set sail for Upernavik, a Danish settlement on the coast of western Greenland. Keeping the land in view, sometimes rowing, sometimes sailing, often endangered by strong gales and heavy falls of snow, they reached their destination safely. But some of the men were weak and frostbitten by this time; Patterson decided to leave them with two whaleboats at Upernavik and push on to the south with the rest. The following day he set out with five whaleboats for Lively, another Danish settlement more than 500 miles from Melville Bay. The intrepid whalermen reached that place on 29 June where they eventually took passage to Orkney on a Danish supply ship. All of the crew of *Lady Jane* survived the experience and arrived at their homes on Tyneside and elsewhere during October. A remarkable story and one of the lesser known epics of Arctic exploration and adventure.

John Patterson was the last of the old whaler captains of north-east England. After the loss of *Lady Jane* he moved to Aberdeen where he commanded other whaleships until 1863. Patterson died at North Shields in 1879 and the last survivor of the crew of *Lady Jane*, James Thompson, also died there in 1915 at the age of 91. Thompson had served as a boatsteerer in several whalers commanded by John Patterson between 1845-1855. The legacy of old Greenlandmen such as these had already been absorbed into a broader fishing tradition long before both men had died. It was also true of the old whalermen of Berwick, Sunderland and Whitby.

Renowned for their toughness and nautical skills, Greenland seamen acquired a kind of folk hero status within their maritime communities. North-East England had long been recognised as a centre for the recruitment of Greenland seamen and some famous whaling families originated in the region. David Gray, the founder of a Peterhead dynasty of whalermen hailed from South Shields; the Sadler's of Hull traced their roots to Cullercoats; the Harrison's of Newcastle, Hull and Hobart, Tasmania originated at Seaton Sluice in Northumberland and Francis Banks, founder of a Whitby whaling family was born at Stockton-on-Tees.

In the century between 1750-1850 all of the principal ports of north-east England engaged ships in the Greenland Whale Fishery. Newcastle and Whitby dominated this local involvement but whalers also sailed from Stockton, Sunderland and Berwick at one time or another. In 1785 the combined fleet of whaling ships sent out from north-east England represented 25 per cent of the national fleet and in 1788 over 50 local ships sailed to the whaling grounds. Although the size of this regional fleet subsequently declined, a commitment to Arctic enterprise endured until the middle of the nineteenth century. In addition to sponsoring the development of whaling skills amongst local merchant seamen, the Greenland trade came to have considerable commercial and economic importance as well. Arctic whalers made heavy demands on port facilities and local whaleships like *Volunteer* of Whitby, *Norfolk* of Berwick or *Lady Jane* of Newcastle became the objects of great pride and affection at their home ports. Their seasonal departures and arrivals were usually witnessed by crowds of spectators who waited anxiously for the slightest news of their progress. Successful voyages produced a carnival-like atmosphere since, as one contemporary writer put it '*...a good Greenland voyage was then the joy of the shore*'. But that joy could just as frequently turn to sorrow as news of the hardship, suffering and death of loved ones in the frozen north filtered back to small and close-knit maritime communities.

In view of these long established connections with whaling enterprise it seems remarkable that little of consequence has been written about it. The only modern, scholarly account is Jackson, G. *The British Whaling Trade* (Adam & Charles Black, London, 1978), which is now over twenty years old. Another basic source is Lubbock, B. *The Arctic Whalers* (Brown Son & Ferguson, Glasgow, 1937). But Lubbock is anecdotal, poorly referenced, often inaccurate and more concerned with the ships than the economics of the trade. Gillies-Ross, W. *Arctic Whalers: Icy Seas*

(Irwin Publishing, Toronto, 1985) relates the customs and conditions of the Davis Straits Fishery based on accounts compiled by officers and surgeons of British whalers. It provides an excellent context for the general reader and might be read in conjunction with other eye-witness accounts such as Credland, A.G. (ed.), *The Journal of Surgeon Cass Aboard the Whaler* Brunswick *of Hull, 1824* (Humberside Library and Arts, Hull, 1988). Another is Barron, W. *Old Whaling Days* (Conway Maritime Press, 1970). The first of these accounts to be associated with a whaler from the region records the experience of two Orkneymen in the crew of *Grenville Bay* of Newcastle during her ice drift voyage of 1836-37. It is contained within Troup, J.A. *The Icebound Whalers* (The Orkney Press, Stromness, 1987).

A number of books published in recent years recount the whaling trade of particular ports. Peterhead is particularly well served in this respect with Buchan, A.R. *The Peterhead Whaling Trade* (The Buchan Field Club Occasional Publications, No.1, Peterhead, 1993) and Sutherland G. *The Whaling Years: Peterhead 1788-1893* (Centre for Scottish Studies, University of Aberdeen, 1993). The premier English port, Hull, has also benefited from a recent publication, Credland, A.G. *The Hull Whaling Trade: An Arctic Enterprise* (Hutton Press Ltd., Beverley, 1995). The whaling trade of Whitby has been popularised by the publication of reprinted material and selections from Scoresby's journals such as *Journal of a Voyage to the Northern Whale Fishery*, originally published in 1823 and T. & C. Stamp, *Greenland Voyager* (Caedmon of Whitby, 1983). William Scoresby's *An Account of the Arctic Regions with a History and Description of the Northern Whale Fishery*, (2 vols., Edinburgh, 1820), is the earliest, comprehensive account of the British Greenland Fishery and remains essential reading for students of Arctic whaling. The Scoresby Archive at Whitby has facilitated the survival of one of the most important collections of material relating to the Greenland Trade. The Scoresbys are probably the only local whaling family whose exploits are widely known and appreciated by the general public. William Scoresby (the younger) achieved international recognition for his contributions to Arctic science and navigation. The Scoresby connection has helped to establish Whitby as the premier whaling port of the region in popular imagination. By contrast the exploits of Scoresby's contemporaries who sailed from Newcastle or Berwick are little known and poorly recorded. A few scattered artefacts have survived the passage of time and circumstance. Descendants of old Greenlandmen have occasionally preserved a record of their ancestors exploits in the Arctic. The George Palmer Collection at Southwold in Suffolk, includes the only surviving run of logbooks of an Arctic whaler which sailed from a port in the region. *Cove* was built at Whitby and sailed from the river Tyne between 1812 and 1833. George Palmer, master of *Cove* was the father of the more well known, Charles Mark Palmer, founder of a shipyard at Jarrow which became something of an industrial legend on Tyneside. The Palmer Collection also includes a number of oil paintings depicting *Cove* whaling in the Davis Straits. Elsewhere, harpoons or whalebone artefacts have occasionally been handed down through the generations and the region still boasts some impressive examples of whalebone arches for those inclined to look for them. They represent a tangible reminder of an age when great whales were an essential resource and whale hunting from open boats in Arctic conditions with primitive, hand-held harpoons was a difficult and dangerous occupation.

The Whaling Trade of North East England 1750-1850 aims to revive an interest in the region's distant whaling connections and provide a context within which this important aspect of the maritime history of north-east England might be understood.

1

'The Newcastle voyage...is the especial nursery and school of seamen...[and]...the gentlest and most open to landsmen'

[Anon, 1615]

Regional Shipping and the Rise of the Greenland Trade

The Coasting Trade

By the middle of the eighteenth century the principal ports of north-east England had become important centres of business and commerce. The growth of the coal trade and the expansion of the Baltic and north European trades in particular, stimulated the development of the regional economy and came to dominate the employment of local shipping. By the end of the century, Whitby, Sunderland and Newcastle were amongst the leading outports in the Kingdom, in terms of their shipping tonnage, and each of them had become important centres of shipbuilding and maritime-related industry. The subsidiary ports of the region, Stockton-on-Tees and Berwick-upon-Tweed, exhibited a similar picture of growth and prosperity.

The pre-eminence of the coal trade and the 'Geordie' brigs that came to be associated with it, is undoubtedly the best known and most enduring aspect of the maritime economy of the region. The coal trade was the largest single activity of coastal shipping during the Industrial Revolution and the majority of vessels built and registered in the North-East were engaged in it.[1] The Great Northern coalfield of Northumberland and Durham was the first British coalfield to be extensively exploited and developed. Although it was remote from the population centres of southern England, it had the distinct advantage of easy access to the sea and, as the demand for coal steadily grew, the coal trade came to provide employment for hundreds of ships. Colliers were generally larger than was usual for vessels engaged in the coasting trades and their size, cargo-carrying capacity and frequency of

Table 1. The six leading ports in the coastal trade of England and Wales, 1760

Port	*Coastal tonage*	*Overseas tonnage*	*Total tonnage*	*% coastal tonnage*
Newcastle	26,618	5,265	31,883	83.5
Sunderland	21,060	10,010	31,070	67.8
Scarborough	12,060	22,820	34,880	34.6
Whitby	10,740	3,470	14,210	75.6
Great Yarmouth	7,140	3,480	10,620	67.2
Hull	5,494	5,670	11,164	49.2

Source: Adapted from Aldcroft and Freeman, *Transport in the Industrial Revolution*, Table 17, p.150

sailings increased as the eighteenth century wore on.[2] In the early 1700s it was common for colliers to be laid up during the months of December to March when winter gales made the east coast a hazardous and inhospitable place. Coal imports into London from the North-East during these winter months amounted to only 6 per cent of the annual total. In 1775, 4,343 coal shipments were cleared from the river Tyne alone and by 1830 there were more than 10,000 voyages in the coal trade from the ports of the region.[3] The colliers of Newcastle and Shields dominated these voyages followed closely by those of Sunderland which had already become Britain's principal port for coal shipped overseas by 1700 despite the unimproved nature of the harbour at that date. The River Wear Commissioners, founded in 1717, steadily improved the navigation and facilities of Sunderland harbour and coal exports doubled between 1750 and 1790. Indeed, of the 392 vessels registered at the port in 1786 over 80 per cent of them were brigs and snows, the commonest rigs in the coal trade.[4]

The importance of Whitby ships in the coal trade was also well established and seems to have developed from its shipowning and shipbuilding traditions as well as in response to a local demand for coal on the north Yorkshire coast. Contemporary local historians of Whitby emphasised the importance of the manufacture of alum as a source of demand for coal shipments.[5] Charlton, for example, writing in 1779, believed that the alum trade at Whitby: '*raised us out of obscurity, made us acquainted with navigation...*'.[6] More recent research has suggested that the connection between the coal trade and the alum industry was probably less important than contemporary writers believed. It is much more likely that cumulative harbour improvements, beginning with the Act of 1702, were more significant in stimulating the growth of a prosperous shipping industry at Whitby.[7] James Cook's well known preference for Whitby built colliers raised few eyebrows at the Admiralty[8] and was, perhaps, the most popular demonstration of Whitby's emergence as a major port of the region.

By the second half of the eighteenth century the Yorkshire coast was one of the most important centres of the British fishing industry. The bulk of the fishing activity was sustained by small coastal communities like Flamborough, Robin Hood's Bay and Staithes. Only Scarborough amongst the harbour ports was a significant fishing station at this date. Surprisingly, despite its size and importance as a centre of maritime trade and industry, Whitby was relatively insignificant as a fishing port. As late as 1817 Whitby had just nine fishermen and three fishmongers.[9] By contrast, Staithes was the largest fishing station on the English east coast north of the Wash. In 1817 this small port operated a fleet of 70 cobles and seventeen five-man boats–3-masted decked fishing luggers up to 53 feet in length.[10] Long lining for cod and haddock during the spring and drifting for herring in late summer and autumn were the mainstay of their activity.

Yarm and Stockton were the principal ports of the river Tees in this period. Small quantities of alum were shipped from Stockton-on-Tees although lead was much more important. Most of the vessels trading from the Tees during the eighteenth century carried lead ingots as part of their general cargoes. The trade of Stockton at this date reflected the extensive hinterland of the port and was dominated by agricultural produce. If our picture of the Tees in 1851, after the arrival of the railway, is one of coal, iron and heavy engineering, a century earlier Stockton was pre-eminently a grain port.

The coastal carriage of grain and other agricultural produce was, after the coal trade, the most significant employer of British shipping during the Industrial Revolution. Grain was more widely distributed than any other product and its movement contributed significantly to the development of regional and interregional trade. With the possible exception of Hull, the coastal grain trade was dominated by small and intermediate ports, principally on the east coast of the British Isles. In north-east England this included Stockton with Hartlepool in the south of the region and Berwick-upon-Tweed with Alnmouth in the north. The trade of the latter ports grew noticeably during the first half of the eighteenth century. Between July 1732 and June 1733, for example, these Northumberland ports combined to export over 50,000 quarters of grain coastwise,[11] and by the end of the century Berwick ranked amongst the top six grain ports in Britain.

Table 2. The coasting trade at Stockton-on-Tees: outward cargoes of selected vessels, January 1752

Ship	*Destination*	*Cargo*
Success	London	470 pieces lead (30 tons); 320 quarters oats; 6 casks tallow; 1 box hard soap; 26 casks pork; 2 boxes apparel; 3 trusses and 1 box English linen; 20 loose hams; 1400 firkins butter
William and Mary	Alloa	550 quarters oats; 4 tons best cheese; 1 small cask hams; 20 boxes apparel; 20 half-firkins British honey; 5 sides bacon; 5 firkins butter
Love	London	1550 pieces lead (92 tons); 36 bolts of British-made sailcloth; 4 hogheads and 170 loose hams; 64 firkins butter; 32 casks pickled cod English caught and cured–duties paid; 1 bundle dried beef; assorted ironmongery; 2 hogheads tallow; 1 hogshead hams; 2 bundles woollen goods.

Source: Stockton Port Books (Coastal), PRO, E/190/252/1.

Berwick's reputation was enhanced by the export of salmon which, from about 1750, was transported to Billingsgate in purpose-built smacks. In their heyday, before 1815, these robust and seaworthy vessels were amongst the fastest sailing ships of their type anywhere in Britain. In addition to their cargoes of salmon, grain, eggs and butter, Berwick smacks like *Queen Charlotte* and *Tweed Packet* also ran a regular passenger service between Leith and London. In favourable conditions they could usually complete the 400-mile voyage in three or four days, and at two guineas for a stern cabin, they were cheaper and generally more comfortable than the Edinburgh-London mail coach.

In the first half of the eighteenth century north-east England also sustained a significant salt-making industry. There were well over 170 salt-pans in operation at North and South Shields by 1700 forming the largest concentration of salt works in Britain at that time.[12] There were numerous other salt-pans at Sunderland, Seaton Sluice and Blyth. Between 1710 and 1730 an annual average of almost 13,000 tons of salt was shipped coastwise from the Tyne, the bulk of it to London and the outports. Manufactured glass products, particularly glass bottles, also figured prominently in the cargoes of coasting ships sailing from the Tyne and Wear.

In north Northumberland, after about 1770, small sloops came to be associated with the carriage of lime from large coastal lime kilns at Seahouses, Beadnell and later Holy Island. Significant quantities of lime were also shipped from Sunderland where the fires from burning kilns were considered to be a danger to navigation. By an Act of 1785 the River Wear Commission was allowed to build protecting walls on the seaward side of the lime kilns because:

> *'the lights...from several lime kilns...have frequently misled Masters, Mariners and Pilots having care of ships and vessels belonging to and using the said port of Sunderland whereby great damage and loss have been and may be occasioned...'*[13]

Most of the lime went to Scottish ports, particularly Perth and Dundee. Industrial lime kilns usually operated on a seasonal basis; the kilns were lit in the spring and extinguished in the autumn when many of the vessels engaged in the trade reverted to the carriage of grain or coal during the winter months.

This, then, was the general picture of the coasting trade of north-east England during the late eighteenth century. Coal and grain were the staples of the region's coastal shipping but the trade of individual ports often reflected a local specialisation; alum at Whitby, lead at Stockton, lime at Sunderland and Seahouses, salmon at Berwick. In addition, fishing continued to sustain the communities of coastal villages like Cullercoats and Cresswell, Runswick Bay and Staithes. The daily sailings of brigs, snows and schooners from the principal ports of the region was mirrored by the movement of numerous open boats, sloops and smacks from minor ports and havens. There could have been few days, particularly during the summer months, when an observer of the coastal waters of north-east England was not impressed by the sight of numerous sails and crowded harbours.

Foreign trade

Foreign trade was not the primary activity of local ships during the eighteenth century. Most of them spent their working lives in the coasting trade. However, even the smallest vessels were capable of undertaking voyages to continental Europe or elsewhere, and the largest vessels did so frequently. Indeed, many local ships came to be associated with a pattern of trading which involved the carriage of different commodities on each leg of a round voyage. The Baltic and Scandinavian trades were especially important in this respect. Typically, a Newcastle or Whitby collier might deliver its cargo in the Thames, sail out to the Baltic in ballast and then return to an east coast port with a cargo of timber, hemp or iron. Some voyaged further afield, into the Mediterranean or even across the north Atlantic. The voyages of *Forrester* of Shields, between 1781 and 1786, outlined in Table 3, demonstrates the flexibility of sailing ship utilisation and the important linkage between the coal trade and the Baltic trade in this period.

Table 3. Voyages performed by the ship *Forrester* of Shields between 1781-1786

Year	*Voyages*	*Cargo*
1781-1782	Shields–London	Coal
	Shields–Lübeck	Coal
	Lübeck–Cronstadt	In ballast
	Cronstadt–Hull	Iron-hemp-tallow
1783	Shields–Wyborg	In ballast
	Wyborg–Newcastle	Deals
	Shields–Cronstadt	Coal
	Cronstadt–Newcastle	Iron-hemp-tallow
1784	Shields–London	Coal
	Several repeat voyages	Coal
	Shields–Archangel	In ballast
	Archangel–Shields	1600 barrels tar
1785	Shields–London	Coal
	London–Memel	In ballast
	Memel–Kings Lynn	Timber
	Shields–Marseilles	Coal
	Marseilles–London	Cotton, sasparilla
1786	Shields–Gibraltar–Algerian port	Coal
	Barbary–Gibraltar	For orders wheat, beeswax and sheep
	Gibraltar–Cadiz	In ballast
	Cadiz–Konigsberg	Salt
	Konigsberg–Memel	In ballast
	Memel–Corunna	Spars
	Corunna–Exmouth–Shields	In ballast

Source: Richardson, W. *A Mariner of England* (Conway Maritime Press, 1970), pp.6-27.

The ports of north-east England had been trading with northern Europe, Scandinavia and the Baltic for centuries. The so-called 'cogs' of the Hanseatic League certainly visited the Tyne during the Middle Ages and when the Company of

Merchant Adventurers of Newcastle was established sometime before 1480, their monopoly of trade in '*train oil and other Baltic products...*'[14] was confirmed by charter.

At the beginning of the eighteenth century Norway rather than the Baltic was the greatest source of timber for the British market. Local sailing ships regularly carried cargoes from Bergen, Drammen and Christiania, ports which had the distinct advantage of being ice-free throughout the year. Most of this Norwegian timber was imported as 'deals'—sawn boards up to 3¼ inches (8 cm) thick, from 7-11 inches (18-28 cm) wide and up to 20 feet (6 m) in length. By contrast, few of the vessels trading into the Baltic before about 1760 carried timber exclusively. For example, during the first week of August 1735, five of the seven vessels arriving in the Tyne from foreign ports, brought cargoes from Norway and the Baltic. *Scheedam Merchant* and *St. Peter* from Bergen, carried timber only, whereas *Industry* brought hemp and iron from St. Petersburg, *Patrick Henry*, iron and deals from Gothenburg, and *Eaden Mary*, iron, deals and tar from Norrköping in Sweden. Fifty years later, the Baltic trade had become the focus of employment for hundreds of sailing ships and vessels from the North-East accounted for over 40 per cent of British shipping passing through The Sound. By the 1780s most vessels were carrying timber exclusively, 'balks' from Memel,[15] spars from Danzig and 'great masts', upwards of half a metre in diameter, felled in the forests of Byelorussia and then floated to Riga for transportation to England. Another advantage of the Baltic trade for local ships was that it was substantially a carrying trade where the port of destination was not always the port of departure as well. Ships sailing with coal from Shields or Sunderland commonly delivered Baltic timber at Hull, Lynn or the naval dockyards at London or Portsmouth. Moreover, since return voyages to the Baltic could be quite short, usually no more than two months, ships engaged in other trades and arriving at their home ports later in the year could also participate in it. Vessels arriving from longer oceanic voyages during August and September, for example, could still undertake a combined coal and Baltic voyage before ice put an end to the sailing season. The opportunity to undertake these late season voyages was of central importance to shipowners who employed their vessels in the Greenland Whale Fishery.

The Greenland Trade

The first indication of an interest in prosecuting the Greenland Whale Fishery from north-east England came from the Tyneside business community in December 1749. The Newcastle newspapers carried a number of advertisements calling for minimum subscriptions of £100 to finance the creation of a local whaling company. Captain Jonathan Blagdon, a master mariner with interests in the American trades, seems to have been the source of these advertisements. But there were no further references to the venture for more than a year. However, in November-December 1751 the Newcastle newspapers again carried a number of advertisements calling for subscriptions to finance the establishment of the Newcastle Whale Fishing Company.[16] A number of prominent local merchants took an interest in the venture on this occasion. Sir Walter Blackett, M.P. for Newcastle between 1734 and 1777 and five times Lord Mayor of the town, led the list of notables who subscribed. Others included the incumbent mayor, Ralph Sowerby, and most of the common councillors and aldermen. The Newcastle Whale Fishing Company was formally established at a general meeting of subscribers on 4 December 1751. A Board of Managers was appointed to conduct the business of the Company.

Although the account books of the Newcastle Company have not survived, a reliable estimate of initial costs can still be made by comparison with other ventures.[17] The Dunbar Company, for example, paid £2,186 on the London market for their 295 ton whaler *North Star* and the Exeter Company, £2,150 for *Exeter*, 346 tons. The Newcastle Company purchased *Swallow*, 297 tons, in December 1751 after a general meeting of the managers had sanctioned a call of 30 per cent on sums already subscribed. If this initial sum represented the purchase price of *Swallow*, which seems likely, and the vessel cost about £2,000, then it may be safely assumed that the Newcastle merchants had subscribed about £6,000 to the venture.[18] The remainder of the money, for fitting out and provisioning, was paid over in March 1752 prior to the vessel's departure from the Tyne. *Swallow* had a successful voyage. She returned to the Tyne in early July 1752 with four sizeable Greenland whales:: '*...uncommon good success...*' reported the *Newcastle Courant* '*...to the general satisfaction of the whole town and neighbourhood which was demonstrated by the ringing of bells...*'[19]

The Newcastle Company got off to a good start and the subscribing merchants were obviously encouraged. They raised further sums of money during the autumn and winter of 1752 and sent three whalers to the Arctic grounds in 1753. *Swallow* was accompanied by *Resolution*, 420 tons, and *Dolphin*, 390 tons. These large vessels became the nucleus of the Newcastle whaling fleet over the following decade.

Whitby merchants also established a Whale Fishing Company and entered two ships into the Greenland trade in 1753, *Sea Nymph* and *Henry and Mary*. Few details about the Whitby Company appear to have survived but it was not as successful as the Company at Newcastle. The combined catch of the Whitby whalers in 1753 was just three whales. Undeterred, Whitby merchants equipped two more whalers in 1754, *Dolphin* and *Anne* and this time they met with better success. *Henry and Mary* took five whales, *Dolphin,* three and *Anne,* two. Successful whale fishing was heavily dependent on the skills and experience of the captain and his crew and evidence

ORIGINAL BOARD OF MANAGERS OF THE NEWCASTLE WHALE FISHING COMPANY

CHAIRMAN: SIR WALTER BLACKETT
SECRETARY: THOMAS AUBONE

John Stevenson	master mariner
John Simpson	merchant
Ralph Sowerby	coal fitter
George Colpitts	coal fitter
Matthew Bell	coal fitter
John Cookson	glass-maker
Aubone Surtees	coal fitter
Robert Carrick	merchant
Peregrine Tyzack	glass-maker
George Headlam	shipbuilder
Ralph Carr	merchant

Source: *Newcastle Chronicle*, 30 November 1751.

suggests that the indifferent performance of the Whitby ships reflected the inexperience of British seamen at this date:

> '*In the early stages of the Greenland trade*', wrote George Young in 1817, '*...harpooners and other officers were procured from Holland as our sailors were then unacquainted with the whale fishing.*'[20]

The muster rolls of these early Whitby whalers certainly indicate the employment of Dutch specialists, but not to the extent that Young suggested. In March 1753 *Sea Nymph* sailed from Whitby with 49 men. None of them were Dutch. The master, James Wilson, came from Sunderland and the mates were from Shields. Only one of the harpooners, Thomas Grey, came from Whitby, most of the others came from London, Shields and Sunderland.[21] The inexperience of these seamen was undoubtedly an important influence on the limited success of the early Whitby whalers and probably persuaded their owners to employ foreign specialists. In 1754 *Sea Nymph* sailed with a mixed crew which included four Dutchmen; three of them mustered as harpooners and the other as an apprentice. *Henry and Mary* carried a single Dutch harpooner, Manken Prudom, between 1754 and 1756 and a Dane, Sven Petersen, mustered on board *Anne* in 1756. All of the remaining seamen were British.[22] It would appear that the employment of foreign seamen at Whitby was minimal and short-lived, although the practice persisted at some Scottish ports well into the 1760s.[23] It was much more significant for the long term future of the whaling trade at Whitby that the crews of these early whalers included seamen who later established themselves as successful local captains. Francis Banks, perhaps the best known of the Whitby whalermen in the pre-Scoresby era, mustered as a line manager and then harpooner of *Sea Nymph* between 1753 and 1756. Another contemporary, Thomas Hodgson, who later commanded whalers at Newcastle and Whitby, mustered as the mate of *Anne*.[24]

Although the establishment of whaling companies was the usual way by which merchants expressed an interest in the Greenland trade at this early stage, a number of large merchant houses also became involved. This was certainly the case at Hull and in London. At Newcastle two of the foremost merchant houses, John Baker & Co. and Edward Mosley & Co., entered vessels into the trade in 1755 and 1756. These were *Robert*, 268 tons and *Phoenix*, 260 tons. Baker and Mosley were aldermen of Newcastle, and sometime Lord Mayors of the town. Both of them had extensive commercial interests. Mosley remained one of the principal shipowners at Newcastle in 1786 and his association with John Baker included their joint investment, together with Aubone Surtees and Ralph Carr, in the Tyne Bank founded in 1772. With the participation of these local merchants Newcastle became the principal outport in the Greenland trade between 1756 and 1765.

The whaling fleet at Newcastle represented a considerable investment. If each vessel was valued at £2,000, and the expenses of manning, provisioning and fitting-out were added, then it is clear that Newcastle merchants were risking as much as £20,000, a very large sum by eighteenth century standards. It represented as much as the investment in the Lombe brothers silk mill in Derby, and far more than was normally invested in a cotton-spinning mill, 20 or even 30 years later. Jedediah Strutt's Belper Mill, for example, cost £5,000 in 1793.[25] Capital sums of this order give some indication of the importance of the shipping industry in mobilising capital. Moreover, since Arctic whalers returned to their home ports with the blubber of the whales they had killed, there was an additional investment in 'Greenland' yards together with their associated wharfs, warehouses and storage facilities. They represented the social overhead capital of the whaling industry.

The secretary of Newcastle Trinity House, Thomas Aubone, was entitled to collect primage from local whaler owners at the rate of 2 pence per tun on their cargoes of bone and blubber. But Aubone, who was also the secretary of the Newcastle Whale Fishing Company, did not always collect the primage impartially. This local tax became a particular source of resentment at Whitby where Newcastle Trinity House claimed a right to levy the tax on the grounds of ancient tradition. Thomas Aubone wrote to John Burgh, the Customs Officer at Whitby, in March 1755:

> *'As nothing has been paid yet from the traders in the Greenland trade for their importation of bone and blubber with you, desire that you will get that mistake rectified...each company here pays primage regularly...'*

The Whitby merchants flatly refused to pay:

> *'I suppose it was looked upon as a very extraordinary thing*', Burgh wrote in reply, '*to demand a duty on bone and blubber which was imported duty free and a very considerable bounty allowed by the crown for the encouragement of the trade...they seem not inclined to pay any duty without some further authority or letter.*'[26]

The matter of primage payments at Whitby, in respect of the whaling trade at least, was never resolved to the satisfaction of Trinity House. Whitby merchants like John Yeoman, refused to pay primage as a matter of principle and considering the indifferent profits of the early years they were hardly likely to change their minds.

The annual earnings of each vessel employed by the Newcastle Company varied from its bounty value, which would represent the only income from an unsuccessful whaling voyage, to more than £5,000 which would represent the value of the cargo obtained by *Resolution* in 1756. The crew of *Resolution* had the good fortune to find themselves amongst a run of whales and her harpooners eventually killed fifteen of them. It was an unprecedented catch by the standards of the time and the cargo provided the basis of a dividend of 20 per cent paid to the shareholders in that year. The Newcastle ships seem to have made profitable voyages in 1752, 1755, 1756, 1759 and 1763. However, there were seven voyages when the same vessels returned 'clean'. *Swallow,* which eventually sailed fifteen voyages to the Arctic during her whaling career, made seven profitable ones, a favourable performance compared to some vessels at other ports. Between 1750 and 1760, for example, 34 of the 127 Scottish whaling voyages were 'clean', about 25 per cent.[27] The first of the Edinburgh ships *Tryall* appears to have been a financial disaster, with eight 'clean' voyages in eleven, and a total catch of only nine whales.

The early Whitby ships were clearly more successful than those at Leith and Dundee but profits remained indifferent and the outbreak of the Seven Years War only exacerbated the situation. French privateers swarmed off the Yorkshire coast in 1757 disrupting the coal trade and the inshore fishing industry alike. Whalers with their large crews and heavy armament were not as vulnerable as the colliers but they began, nevertheless, to sail from Whitby and Newcastle in armed squadrons:

> '*they are completely fitted with great guns and small arms*' went one report in the *Newcastle Journal* '*...and are to act in concert with Mr. Brown as commodore...if any French privateer should have the assurance to attack them 'tis presumed he will meet with a warm reception...*'[28]

Armed or otherwise these whalers could not always protect themselves from the fury of Arctic storms. Whitby lost *Leviathan* in 1758 and Newcastle *Phoenix* and *Resolution* in 1760. It was time to take stock. Whitby merchants decided to abandon the trade in 1761 and did not take it up again until 1767. The Newcastle Whale Fishing Company persevered with moderate success until their remaining ships, *Dolphin* and *Swallow* were themselves wrecked in 1763 and 1766. The Company ceased trading soon afterwards. By 1766 the future of the Greenland trade lay with independent merchants not with whale fishing companies although several Scottish concerns survived well into the 1770s. At Newcastle, John Baker & Co. continued to be the most important merchant house involved with the trade. Amongst the more prominent of the 'new' merchants was Francis Hurry (1729-1808) who was the first representative of the Hurry family of Great Yarmouth to begin building ships at Howdon-on-Tyne in 1758. He was responsible for building a large graving dock there, and between 1770 and 1805 Howdon dockyard became one of the best known in England. Francis Hurry regularly built ships for the Admiralty and the East India Company and supplied a growing local demand for ships. In May 1758 he married a daughter of Thomas Airey, a hostman of Newcastle, and they jointly took an interest in Greenland whaling about 1764. On the foreshore, on the east side of Howdon burn were facilities for bone cleaning and blubber boiling. There were also extensive storage facilities for the paraphernalia of whaling–harpoons, lines, utensils and casks. Their first ship, *Newcastle*, 340 tons, had originally been owned by John Baker & Co. who used her as a replacement for *Phoenix*. But *Newcastle* was not a successful ship. She experienced three 'clean' voyages in four between 1761 and 1764. Ironically, it was fire rather than ice that ended the short and unsuccessful career of this large Tyne whaler. In March 1766, *Newcastle* was burnt down to the waterline in a spectacular conflagration which at one point even threatened to destroy some of the thatched cottages on Howdon shore. Undeterred, Hurry and Airey introduced *John and Margaret*, a large American built ship to the Greenland trade as a replacement. *John and Margaret* became one of the stalwarts of the Tyne whaling fleet for almost half a century. Two other vessels, *Royal Exchange* and *Annabella*, also joined the local whaling fleet during these years, in 1763 and 1765.

Despite the arrival of these vessels Newcastle lost its position as the leading outport and fleet numbers declined to such an extent that only two vessels sailed from the river Tyne in 1774. *Annabella* completed only three voyages before she was crushed between two ice-floes and wrecked in May 1768. Her crew was saved by *Henrietta* of London and *James and Mary* of Whitby.[29] It was some compensation, perhaps, that another Newcastle whaler, *Royal Exchange* with a cargo of twelve whales and 2,300 seals and *Jenny* of Whitby with nine whales, 570 seals and four polar bears(!) were the most successful vessels in the British whaling fleet that year. *Royal Exchange* was herself wrecked in 1773. The re-emergence of Whitby as a whaling port and the slow decline of Newcastle became a feature of the years after 1766 as the focus of local whaling enterprise shifted to the north Yorkshire coast.

References

1. Aldcroft, D. and Freeman, M. *Transport in the Industrial Revolution*, (Manchester University Press, 1983), p.155.

2. For a full discussion of the increasing productivity of North-East collier ships, see Ville, S. 'Total Factor Productivity in the English Shipping Industry: The North-East Coal Trade, 1700-1850', *Economic History Review*, 2nd series, XXXIX, 3, (1986), pp.355-370

3. Flinn, M.W. *The History of the British Coal Industry*, (Oxford University Press, 1984), II, p.172.

4. Customs Port Shipping Registers, Sunderland. Tyne-Wear Archives Dept. (TWAD), Ex/Sul/1/1.

5. Alum was widely used as a fixing agent in dyeing and tanning and had been manufactured on the north Yorkshire coast since the beginning of the seventeenth century. A number of interesting articles about the Alum Trade have been published in *The Dalesman* magazine. See, for example, Raistrick, A. 'The Alum Industry', April, May, June, 1950; Barton, P. 'The Alum Ships', March 1969.

6. Charlton, L. *A History of Whitby*, (1779), p.307.

7. The significance of the coal trade to the development of Whitby during the eighteenth century is fully discussed in Jones, S. 'A Maritime History of the Port of Whitby, 1714-1914', University of London, Ph.D. (1982).

8. Hausman, W.J. 'Size and Profitability of English Colliers in the Eighteenth Century', *Business History Review*, LI, 4 (1977), pp.460-473.

9. Robinson, R. *A History of the Yorkshire Coast Fishing Industry 1780-1914* (Hull University Press, 1987), p.8.

10. Robinson, *Yorkshire Coast Fishing Industry*, p.10.

11. Berwick Port Books (Coastal), Public Record Office (PRO), E190/173/12 and 13 and 174 /1 and 2.

12. Ellis, J. 'The Decline and Fall of the Tyneside Salt Industry, 1660-1790: A Reappraisal', *Economic History Review*, 33, (Feb. 1980), pp.45-58.

13. Miller, S. 'The River Wear Commission, 1717-1859', *Antiquities of Sunderland*, XXVII, (1977-79), pp.57-68.

14. Fraser, C.M. and Emsley, K. *Tyneside*, (David and Charles, 1973) p.26.

15. 'Balks' was a term used to denote lengths of squared timber.

16. See, for example, *Newcastle Journal*, 23 November 1751.

17. These are the Exeter Whale Fishing Company account books (1754-59), the costs incurred by the East Lothian and Merse Whale Fishing Company of Dunbar (1752) and the establishment and subsequent profitability of the Edinburgh Whale Fishing Company.

18. The East Lothian and Merse Whale Fishing Company had an initial capital sum of £6,000 and the Exeter Company £5,000.

19. *Newcastle Courant*, 11 July 1752.

20. Young, Revd. G. *A History of Whitby*, (1817), p.563.

21. The muster roll of *Sea Nymph*, 1753, can be found in the Appendix.

22. Muster rolls of *Sea Nymph*, No. 93, 1753 and No. 54, 1754; *Henry and Mary*, No. 94, 1753, No. 232, 1754; *Dolphin*, No. 233, 1754; *Anne*, No. 69, 1754, Whitby Literary and Philosophical Society (WLPS).

23. At Dunbar, for example, *North Star* was still sailing with Dutch harpooners as late as 1770. Scottish Record Office (SRO), E508/67/8.

24. Muster rolls of *Sea Nymph*, No. 93, 1753; No. 54, 1754; No. 270, 1755; No. 307, 1756 and *Anne*, No. 69, 1754; No. 62, 1756, WLPS.

25. Matthias, P. *The First Industrial Nation* (Methuen & Co., 1969), p.131.

26. TWAD, GU/TH/224.

27. Jackson, G. 'Government Bounties and the Establishment of the Scottish Whaling Trade', *Scottish Themes—Essays in Honour of Professor S.G.E. Lythe* (Scottish Academic Press, 1976), p.55.

28. *Newcastle Journal*, 16 April 1757.

29. Lubbock, B. *The Arctic Whalers* (Brown Son and Ferguson, 1937), p.106.

2

'...follow them among the tumbling mountains of ice and behold them penetrating into the deepest frozen recesses of Hudson's Bay and Davis Straits...'

[Edmund Burke 'On Conciliation with the Colonies', 22 March 1775]

Whaling and the American War, 1770-1783

The emergence of Whitby as the major whaling port of the region and the relative decline of Newcastle, was a noticeable trend in the whaling effort of north-east England during the 1770s. With a large stock of good, second-hand ships and a healthy Baltic trade, Whitby was ideally placed to exploit the opportunities offered by the Greenland trade. Newly built ships were rarely used for whaling purposes and before the construction of steam whalers during the second half of the nineteenth century, few ships were purpose-built for it. Even those that were, rarely incorporated features that could not be built into existing vessels. Whitby-built ships were renowned for their strength and quality of construction. William Scoresby, who had two ships purpose-built in 1812 and 1820[1], believed that Greenland ships:

> *'...should admeasure 3-400 tons; built of the best and strongest material. Flush-decked; hold beams laying low the better to resist a pressure of ice. A flat-floored burdensome hold, for good stowage and carrying a large cargo...'*[2]

Government regulations also had a decisive influence on the choice of ship. The various Bounty Acts required whalers to be: '*...strongly built and a proper ship for such voyage and fishery...*'.[3]

This usually involved the internal strengthening and external fortification of the hull by a technique known as 'doubling' and 'fortifying'. Doubling involved the construction of additional planking to the exterior of the frame of timbers. According to Scoresby, it generally consisted of the application of 2-2½ inches thick oak planking near the bows diminishing to 1 inch near the stern. Whalers, effectively, had double hulls, and many of them also carried large iron 'ice-plates' at the bows just on and slightly below the waterline. Fortifying involved the internal strengthening of the stern and bows by the insertion, at 90° to the axis of the frame, 4 x 12 inches square and 25 feet long oak beams known as 'ice-beams'. The expense of doubling and fortifying accounted for a significant amount of the fitting-out costs and it is unlikely that any vessel would have been permitted to sail from a British port without these additional strengthening features. Owners may have jeopardized their entitlement to the bounty payments and rendered their ships uninsurable had they done so. At the same time, doubling and fortifying did not hinder the usefulness of the vessel for other trades and may also go some way to explaining why some ships became so well established as whalers. The famous Hull whaler *Truelove* is, perhaps, the best known. *Truelove*, built at Philadelphia in 1764, undertook a total of 74 voyages to the Arctic. She was the last sailing whaler in commission when she was eventually withdrawn from the trade in 1868. There were also some notable veterans amongst the whalers of north-east England. The Tyne whaler *John and Margaret* spent 42 years whaling from Howdonpans (1766-1808), while another, *Lady Jane*, worked for 45 years from Willington Quay (1804-1849). At Whitby, *Volunteer* and *Henrietta* eventually completed over 100 voyages to the Arctic between them.[4]

Volunteer, owned by Richard Moorsom and built at Whitby in 1756, was one of a number of ships associated with the revival of Whitby whaling after 1767. An account of her maiden whaling voyage '*An authentick Narration of all the Occurances, in a Voyage to Greenland in the Year 177 2*' was subsequently written and published by William Kidd, the '*Gentleman, Surgeon of the said Ship*'. Kidd's journal is the earliest published account of a voyage to Greenland by an English whaler, and contains valuable information about the wages and working conditions of the men. She carried a crew of 40 men, the majority recruited from Whitby and neighbouring settlements such as Staithes, Sleights and Robin Hood's Bay.

Volunteer sailed from Whitby in a fair S.W. breeze on 24 March 1772 in company with *Jenny*, *James and Mary*, *Hope* and *Porpoise*. She sighted Shetland on 29 March and bore up with the intention of reaching Lerwick but was prevented from doing so by strong northerly gales. On 9 April in latitude 67°47'N:

> *'All on a sudden, about four o'clock in the morning, we were seized with a sudden gale from the north...which put us in the greatest extremity, it being impossible for any man to handle a sail; we continued in this deplorable condition until twelve o'clock, when the storm abated a little, then we got our foresail reeved and our mainsail smothered; in this condition we continued until*

the 10th, when this severe gale had pretty much abated...but the sea desperately high and a very intense frost with showers of snow at intervals...'[5]

After two more severe gales, *Volunteer* joined the main body of the whaling fleet off Spitzbergen on 3 May. On 21 May, in company with the Edinburgh ships *Leith* and *Royal Bounty*, the crew of *Volunteer* sighted their first whales off the Greenland coast amongst heavy drift ice. Another Whitby ship, *Porpoise*, was wrecked nearby only a few days later. The crew of *Volunteer* received the information on 29 June from *Leviathan* of Liverpool. *Volunteer* was still 'clean' at that time and the surgeon pessimistic: '*we have seen no fish since the 14th*', he wrote, '*no hopes of getting into the ice...and the season far spent...*'.[6] *Volunteer*'s luck changed in early July:

> '*Monday, 6 July*
> *At 2 o'clock in the morning, we let fall all of our boats and in about half an hour after Richard Grice got fast to a fish and was soon seconded by all our boats with four boats from the* Dolphin *(of Liverpool) who was very neighbourly in assisting us. We killed it in about an hour...the whalebone 10'2".*'

> '*Thursday, 9 July*
> *About 2 o'clock in the morning we saw some fish and instantly lowered down two boats and came up with a fish that was just dying. Jacob Grimes struck a harpoon into it which secured it as our property [when] the* Dolphin's *boat was not a hundred yards off it...*'

During the afternoon of the same day *Volunteer* anchored in Maklina Bay on the coast of eastern Greenland in latitude 80°20'N. There were already three other ships in the bay, Kidd's journal continued:

> '*Here we begun to put our blubber into casks which employed all the hands. It is the hardest work belonging to the Greenland fishery. At 6 o'clock we weighed anchor and put to sea in company with the* Dolphin *of Liverpool and several other ships...we had not been above four hours at sea before Richard Grice struck a fish, which was killed in about an hour*'.

The crew of *Volunteer* harpooned and killed two more whales before they set sail for Whitby, the last of them '*proved to be more superior than any of the former four [with] 15 inches and a half thick of fat or blubber*'.[7] Kidd was triumphant and computed the value of the cargo '*at near £4,000*'. Not surprisingly, perhaps, the surgeon's estimate proved to be an optimistic one. With oil selling at £18 per tun and whalebone at £350,[8] *Volunteer*'s cargo of 65 tuns of oil and three tons of whalebone was actually worth about £2,220, exclusive of the bounty. But it was a successful voyage by the standards of the period. With wages and fitting-out costs of about £5 per ton,[9] the owner of *Volunteer*, Richard Moorsom, probably made a profit in the region of £1,250. The crew would certainly have considered it a successful voyage as well. Table 4 records the monthly rates and bonus payments paid to the crew of *Volunteer*. Translated into wages it meant that the mate, Matthew Smith, received almost £40 for a five-month voyage and the successful harpooners, Richard Grice, Jacob Grimes and John Brown, between £32-£33.[10]

The outbreak of the American Revolutionary War in 1775 transformed the economic environment of the shipping industry and presented shipowners with new opportunities for the employment of their vessels. Some chose to continue their ships in trade and were able to use higher wartime freight rates to offset increased insurance and wage costs. Others sought to engage their ships in government service as hired transports. At Whitby some of the leading shipowners not only decided to continue their vessels in the whaling trade but even to expand their involvement in it, despite the additional dangers presented by press-gangs and privateers. Even Sunderland merchants dabbled briefly with the trade when they dispatched the aptly named *Hazard* to the whaling grounds between 1774 and 1776.

Table 4. Wages per month and bonus payments paid to the crew of *Volunteer*, 1772

Position	*Monthly rate (£)*	*Fish money (£)*	*Oil money (£)*
Mate	3-10-0	10-6	not recorded
Surgeon	3-10-0	1-1-0	-
Carpenter	3-10-0	10-6	not recorded
Second mate/harpooner	2-10-0	10-6	5-3
Carpenter's mate	2-10-0	5-0	not recorded
Boatsteerer	2-0-0	5-0	"
Line manager	1-15-0	2-6	"
Cook	1-10-0	2-6	"
Seaman	1-10-0	2-6	"

Source: Sowler, G, *Voyage to Greenland in the Year 1772.*

Another Sunderland ship, *Noble Ann*, whose crew later came to be associated with the most notorious press-gang incident to occur on the coast of north-east England during the American War, joined a small fleet of Tyne whalers in 1775. The combined fleet of whalers fitted-out from the region during the American Revolutionary War represented 20-30 per cent of the national total. Whitby ships alone accounted for between 15-22 per cent of the fleet (see Table 5). The cumulative experience of local 'Greenlanders' quickly focused on Whitby as ships and seamen shifted their base of operations to the Esk. Three of the principal officers who sailed in *Volunteer* in 1772 now had the opportunity of commanding their own ships. Matthew Smith who had been the mate, took command of *Delight* in 1774, while two of the harpooners, Jeremiah Boyes and John Brown were given command of *Hercules* and *Freelove* in 1775. There was also something of an exodus of whaling expertise from Shields. John Lattimer, for example, who had acquired his whaling skills on the Tyne ships *Robert* and *Priscilla* during the 1760s assumed command of *Loyal Club* at Whitby in 1774. This ship was already a well-established whaler. She had originally been owned by the Exeter Whale Fishing Company and began sailing to Greenland about 1756.[11] Another 'import' from Shields was George Ismay,

Table 5. Number of Greenland whalers fitted-out at North-East ports during the American Revolutionary War, 1775-1783

	Ports				
Year	*Whitby*	*Sunderland*	*Newcastle*	*National total*	*% North-East*
1775	14	1	3	105	17
1776	15	1	4	98	20
1777	14	-	4	84	21
1778	14	-	4	76	24
1779	14	-	4	62	29
1780	10	-	4	56	25
1781	8	-	4	39	31
1782	7	-	3	43	23
1783	7	-	3	51	20

Source: PRO, BT 6/93/98, 126. Adapted from Jackson, G. *The British Whaling Trade*, Appendix 2.

Table 6. Performance of the Whitby whaling fleet, 1777

Date arrived	*Ship*	*Master's name*	*From*	*Importer's name*	*Cargo* Blubber (butts)	*Cargo* Whalebone (tons)
10 June	*Marlborough*	T. Franks	Davis Straits	H.W. Yeoman & Co.	228	4-00
13 June	*Freelove*	J. Brown	"	Wakefield, Simpson & Co.	340	6-15
12 July	*Speedwell*	J. Steward	"	Thomas Holt	270	6-10
12 July	*Addison*	F. Banks (Snr.)	"	H.W. Yeoman & Co.	284	5-10
14 July	*Friendship*	G. Ismay	"	James Atty & Co.	226	5-10
21 July	*Providence & Nancy*	F. Banks (Jnr.)	"	C. Franklin	204	4-00
22 July	*Delight*	M. Smith	Greenland	R. Moorsom	139	2-00
29 July	*Hercules*	J. Boyes	"	C. Lightfoot & Co.	53	1-00
29 July	*Loyal Club*	J. Lattimer	"	R. Strong & Co.	89	2-00
29 July	*Perseverence*	J. Carling	"	H.W. Yeoman & Co.	40	-15
29 July	*James and Mary*	T. Hodgson	"	J. Yeoman	10	-50
1 Aug.	*Volunteer*	W. Coulson	"	R. Moorsom	190	3-00
1 Aug.	*Henrietta*	W. Cole	"	N. Piper	85	1-10

Source: An Account of Primage duty received for the Trinity House at Newcastle from 5 January 1777–5 January 1778. TWAD, GU/TH/221/17.
Note: Although fourteen ships sailed from Whitby in 1777, only thirteen of them are recorded in the Primage Accounts. The missing vessel appears to be *Providence* which may have been wrecked or captured. All of the whaler owners at Whitby refused to pay the Primage duty.

formerly master of *John and Margaret*, who took *Friendship* from Whitby to the Davis Straits in 1776. All of the principal officers in Ismay's crew, with the exception of the mate, Nicholas Hodgson, came from Shields and Newcastle; the majority had served with him on *John and Margaret* the year before.[12] The Whitby muster rolls reveal numerous other examples.[13]

Many of these men pioneered the shift from the older and increasingly over-exploited Greenland grounds to the Davis Straits. By 1777 the Whitby fleet was equally divided between the two (see Table 6). Moreover, a steady decline in national fleet numbers generally improved the productivity of the ships that remained. Of course, this was not always the case. On the Tyne, for example, the two Davis Straits ships, *Priscilla* and *John and Margaret* met with limited success. The productivity of *Priscilla* marginally improved, but *John and Margaret* after a good first voyage, returned 'clean' in 1777, 1778 and 1779, so that the average catch of the vessel actually declined.[14]

The experience of the Whitby whalers was more positive. In 1777, not an exceptional year, all of the Davis Straits ships secured valuable cargoes. Moreover, despite their longer voyages, they all returned to Whitby before the Greenland ships, two of them before the middle of June. All of the Davis Straits ships obtained significantly greater cargoes. Table 7 represents the estimated earnings and profitability of Henry Walker Yeoman's ships compared to those fitted-out by Richard Moorsom, which sailed to Greenland. Moorsom's whalers were considerably more successful than the other Greenland ships at Whitby. The best 'fished' of the Davis Straits ships was *Freelove* with 113 tuns of whale oil and almost seven tons of whalebone, a cargo worth more than £5,000, including the bounty. Few whaler owners could expect to make this kind of money on any regular basis. *Freelove*, at 341 tons, was one of Whitby's largest whalers and may well have been one and the same ship in which James Cook served his apprenticeship. She was built at Yarmouth in 1746 and eventually completed over fifteen voyages to the Arctic from Whitby before she was withdrawn from the trade in 1792. *Freelove* and *Marlborough* were among a number of Whitby whalers to sail with a 'Letter of Marque' during the American War. Well-armed and heavily manned whaling ships such as these usually had little difficulty in qualifying for Admiralty licences. In 1778 the Whitby whalers sailed together as an armed squadron. But taking precautions against privateers was not the only problem confronting whaler owners. The entry of the French into the war on the side of the American colonists in February 1778 and the declaration of Spain in the following year over-stretched British resources and threatened to disrupt the management of naval operations. The First Lord of the Admiralty, the Earl of Sandwich, was well aware of the implications of the crisis and expressed his

Table 7. Estimated profit and earnings of selected Whitby whalers, 1777

Oil (tuns)	*Bone (cwt.)*	*Oil value (£)*	*Bone value (£)*	*Bounty value (£)*	*Total earnings (£)*	*Estimated expenses (£)*	*Estimated profits (£)*
Ship: *Marlborough*, 228 tons–Davis Straits H.W. Yeoman							
76	80	1,900	1,120	342	3,362	1,140	2,222
Ship: *Addison*, 280 tons*–Davis Straits H.W. Yeoman							
95	110	2,375	1,540	420	4,335	1,400	2,935
Ship: *Delight*, 280 tons*–Greenland R. Moorsom							
46	40	1,150	560	420	2,130	1,400	730
Ship: *Volunteer*, 305 tons–Greenland R. Moorsom							
63	60	1,575	840	457	2,872	1,525	1,347

Notes and Sources: Oil prices £25 per tun, whalebone £280 per ton in PRO, BT 6/93/237–see also Jackson, G. *The British Whaling Trade*, Appendix 7. A bounty of £1-10-0 per ton was paid between 1777-81.

* The tonnage of these vessels is not known and an average has been used. See PRO, BT 6/93 folios 225-26, also Jones, S. 'A Maritime History of the Port of Whitby, 1714-1914', University of London, Ph.D, (1982), Chap.5, Table 1, p.300. Expenses of £5 per ton have been used. PRO, BT 6/93/94. Quantities of oil and bone obtained by each ship is based on the Primage Account returns (see Table 6). A standard conversion of 3 butts=1 tun has been used.

anxieties to Lord North:

> '...*out of 50 ships which is in our whole stock at present, only 41 can be said to be in readiness and some men are wanted even for their equipment, the others cannot be got to sea without some extraordinary measures are used for raising seamen*...'[15]

The situation deteriorated during the course of the year. The crisis of manning called for the recruitment of experienced seamen and a general press, to include all protected seamen, was central to the several schemes of recruitment proposed in June 1779:

> '*What think you of taking the Greenlanders*', the Attorney-General, Lord Thurlow wrote to Sandwich '...*under a promise to return them before the season for fishing?*'[16]

The Admiralty responded quickly to this suggestion and ordered naval officers commanding warships together with those employed on the Impress Service to ignore all the protections it had issued to different categories of mariners, watermen and river workers. The effect on the maritime communities of north-east England was immediate:

> *'The present impress for seamen of all distinctions...has been general throughout the kingdom. A total stop is put to the navigation of this river [Tyne] and the river Wear at Sunderland as many of the keelmen at both places have been impressed...every ship that enters our harbour is immediately boarded and stripped of men and boys...since the impress broke out here it is supposed that upwards of 600 men have been taken.'*[17]

At sea some of the earliest victims of the emergency were the crews of local whaling ships. On 4 July, Independence Day ironically, *Adamant*, bound to Whitby, became the first of many local whalers to confront naval ships off the coast of north-east England. A boat's crew from *Adamant* was intercepted and pressed by H.M. sloop *Fury* while attempting to make their escape at Hartlepool. Attempts by *Fury* to press the remainder of *Adamant*'s crew were fiercely resisted.[18] But the Greenlanders' defiance was short lived. *Fury* followed the Whitby whaler along the Yorkshire coast and '*as soon as the* Adamant *arrived at Whitby Road, H.M. sloop* Fury *and the* Advice *armed tender boarded her and impressed all her hands...*'.[19] The most serious confrontation occurred at the end of the month.

Two of the Newcastle whalers, *Kitty* and *Noble Ann* arrived off the Tyne on 30 July. *Kitty*'s men, clearly aware of the danger they were in, managed to get ashore on the Northumberland coast and thereby avoided a confrontation with the press-gang at Shields. The crew of *Noble Ann* may well have planned to do the same, but they were unable to get close enough inshore before they attracted the attention of the Navy. As *Noble Ann* entered the river Tyne she was surrounded by boats from *Syren*, a new frigate then fitting-out at Shields, boats from the Rendezvous, and several press tenders anchored in the river. The crew of *Noble Ann* refused to surrender themselves and resisted all attempts by the press-gang to stop and board their vessel. The violent confrontation that followed left two men dead and a third seriously wounded. It was undoubtedly the most serious clash between Greenland seamen and the press-gang during the American Revolutionary War. The principal naval officer involved, Edmund Dod, was advised by John Bover, Regulating Captain at Newcastle:

> *'that you are in the utmost danger of your life if you stay at Shields a single day...[for] it is clear that you will immediately be taken up, tried and condemned for wilful murder...'* [20]

Dod accepted Bover's advice and left Shields in the early hours of 2 August. He did not rejoin his ship in the Thames until 5 September. Dod was never brought to trial for the deaths of the Greenland seamen.[21]

Another memorable, though less notorious incident of the American War, involved *Freelove* of Whitby. On 15 August, homeward bound from the Davis Straits, *Freelove* was stopped in Alnmouth Bay by *Content* armed ship, which was intent on pressing her hands:

> '*while on that service...*' recorded the logbook of *Content* '*...two French frigate-built ships bore down and began a brisk fire on us which we returned. Engaged both the French ships till about twelve minutes after two when they being sick of it, run away...we had one killed and four wounded...*' [22]

When the story reached the local newspapers the crew of *Freelove* came in for criticism:

> '*if the Greenlandmen had supported us*', went one account, '*we would probably have brought them both into Shields, but being afraid of herself she came close inshore...*' [23]

But *Content* had already pressed 30 of *Freelove*'s crew leaving her considerably undermanned for such an engagement. Moreover, the master John Brown would have his owners to answer to for any loss or damage to the ship and her cargo. Soon after the engagement *Content* sighted five other Whitby whalers and convoyed them to the Esk, where she impressed seamen from all of them.

The majority of these 'Greenlanders' were released in time to return to their home ports for the beginning of the 1780 season. But fewer ships sailed to the whaling grounds as the wartime situation deteriorated and many owners decided that the attendant risks were not worth the investment. Some of them took the easy way out and hired their whaling ships to the government as transports at remunerative rates.[24] At Whitby the whaling fleet declined by half in two years. Ships like *Jenny* and *Loyal Club* were employed in supplying stores to the army in America. *Noble Ann* was similarly employed. She sailed with coal and other stores for the garrison in Gibraltar, where she was wrecked in April 1781.

The owners of the remaining ships at Newcastle and Whitby persevered. With prices high and the number of whalers comprising the national fleet lower than at any time since 1766 their determination paid dividends. In 1782 and 1783, the Newcastle ships obtained 47 whales. Twenty-nine of these, representing almost 62 per cent of the total, were caught by one ship, *Kitty*, on the old Greenland whaling grounds. The master of *Kitty* was John Lattimer, who had moved back to Shields from Whitby after *Loyal Club* was placed in the Transport Service. Table 8 presents a breakdown of the monetary value of the catches obtained by the

Table 8. Catch and estimated earnings of the Tyne whaling fleet, 1782

Vessel	*Catch (whales)*	*Oil (tuns)*	*Bone (cwt.)*	*Oil value (£)*	*Bone value (£)*	*Bounty value @ £2/ton*	*Total value (£)*	*Estimated profit (£)*
John and Margaret	6	130	100	3,380	1,725	794	5,899	3,914
Priscilla	10	150	140	3,900	2,415	694	7,009	5,274
Kitty	12	144	100	3,744	1,725	702	6,171	4,416

Notes and Sources: Oil price £26 per tun, whalebone £345 per ton in PRO BT 6/93/133 and Jackson, G. *The British Whaling Trade*, Appendix 7. Expenses of £5 per ton have been used. PRO BT 6/93/94.

Newcastle ships in 1782. Hitherto few of the Tyne fleet had experienced this order of success, or were ever to do so again. *John and Margaret*, for example, which had never earned more than £2,760 in any of her sixteen previous voyages to the Arctic, earned twice that sum in 1782.[25] Similarly, *Priscilla*'s voyage proved to be the best of her long career as a whaler, and at Whitby the owners of *Henrietta* shared a profit of over £1,500 in 1782 and 1783.[26]

The return of peacetime conditions in 1783 transformed the situation and stimulated a rapid expansion of British whaling. Well established whaling ports like Newcastle and Whitby reacted quickly to the new commercial circumstances and ships from other local ports soon joined the rush. In 1787, 50 whalers sailed to the Arctic grounds from the ports of north-east England.

References

1. These were *Esk* (354 tons) built at Whitby by Fishburn and Broderick and *Baffin* (321 tons) built at Liverpool by Mottershead and Hayes.

2. Stamp,T. & C. *Greenland Voyager* (Caedmon ofWhitby, 1983), p.2.

3. 26 Geo III. c.41.

4. Numerous other local vessels accumulated more than twenty voyages, such as *Norfolk* of Berwick (1803-1837) and *Grenville Bay* of Newcastle (1816-1840). Additionally, since many whaling ships were subsequently sold between ports,

a number that began their whaling careers from north-east England spent many years in the trade elsewhere. These included *Horn* of Sunderland, *Resolution* of Whitby and *Lord Gambier* of Newcastle which ended their careers at Dundee, Aberdeen and Kirkaldy in 1852, 1830 and 1862 respectively.

5. Sowler, G. *Voyage to Greenland in the Year 1772* (Durham, 1772), p.3.

6. Sowler, *Voyage to Greenland*, p.29.

7. Sowler, *Voyage to Greenland*, p.41.

8. Public Record Office (PRO), BT 6/93/137.

9. PRO, BT 6/93/94.

10. The muster roll of *Volunteer*, 1772 can be found in the Appendix.

11. In July 1756 she was reported to have captured thirteen whales; in 1757 she returned to Topsham 'clean'. See *Newcastle Journal*, 10 July 1756 and 6 August 1757.

12. Muster rolls of *John and Margaret* PRO, BT 98/127 No.165, 1775 and *Friendship* Whitby Literary and Philosophical Society (WLPS), No. 84, 1776. The muster roll of *Friendship*, 1776 can be found in the Appendix.

13. Perhaps the most notable was Thomas Hodgson, who was a veteran by this date. This was the same man who had mustered as the mate of *Anne* at Whitby in 1756, and who subsequently commanded *Royal Exchange* at Shields between 1763-1773. Hodgson commanded *Two Sisters* in 1775 and subsequently, after 1776, *James and Mary*. Another Shields man, Thomas Frank, Jnr., assumed command of Henry Walker Yeoman's ship *Marlborough* in 1777.

14. Barrow, A. 'North East Coast Whale Fishery, 1750-1850', University of Northumbria, Ph.D. (1989), Table 9.2, p.102.

15. Lord Sandwich to Lord North, 6 March 1778 (Sandwich Papers, Navy Records Society), I, p.350.

16. Lord Thurlow to Lord Sandwich, 21 June 1779 (Sandwich Papers, Navy Records Society), III, p.21.

17. *Newcastle Chronicle*, 3 July 1779.

18. Logbook of H.M. sloop *Fury*, PRO, ADM 51/359. Entry for 4 July 1779.

19. *Newcastle Weekly Chronicle*, 10 July 1779.

20. John Bover, Impress Officer at Newcastle, to Captain Edmund Dod, 1 August 1779, PRO, ADM 7/300.

21. A full account of the 'Noble Ann Affair' can be found in Barrow, T. (Ed.) *Press- gangs and Privateers, Aspects of the Maritime History of N.E. England, 1760-1815* (Bewick Press, 1993), pp.13-22.

22. Logbook of *Content* armed ship PRO, ADM 51/209. Entry for 15 August 1779.

23. *Newcastle Chronicle*, 21 August 1779.

24. The rate was £1 per ton per month. See Jackson, G. *Whaling Trade*, p.68.

25. In 1768, *John and Margaret* had obtained five whales and 2,000 seals.

26. Account books of the whaler *Henrietta* of Whitby, National Maritime Museum (NMM), AMS/35.

3

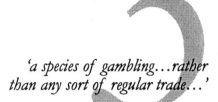

'a species of gambling...rather than any sort of regular trade...'

[William Wilberforce, 12 April 1786]

Boom and Bust: The Whaling Trade of North-East England, 1783-1798

Historians in general and those of the shipping industry in particular are especially interested in the economic effects of the various wars of the eighteenth century. It was the age of industrialisation and as the British economy grew so too did the demand for ships and the port facilities necessary to handle them. Peace with America in 1783 worked to the advantage of British shipowners in a number of different ways. It was especially important to whaler owners because it removed at a stroke their principal competitors in the supply of an expanding oil market.

In 1775 the Greenland Fishery supplied just 15 per cent of the whale oil sold on the British market. By contrast, the New England colonies provided 47 per cent. Ten years later, in 1785, the situation was completely reversed with 46 per cent derived from the Greenland Fishery but only 10 per cent from New England. Imports of whale oil from the United States ceased altogether after 1791.[1]

The American War also compromised the Dutch and contributed significantly to a decline in the number of vessels they sent to the Arctic grounds after 1783. This combination of circumstances left the procurement and supply of whale products almost entirely in the hands of British merchants and they moved quickly to exploit their advantage. The number of Greenland whalers sailing from British ports increased five-fold between 1783 and 1787, from 51 to 250 ships.

The expansion of interest on the north-east coast mirrored the growth of the national fleet. At Newcastle and Whitby experienced shipowners with well-

Table 9. Number of ships committed to whaling from north-east England, 1783-1793

Port	*1783*	*1784*	*1785*	*1786*	*1787*	*1788*	*1789*	*1790*	*1791*	*1792*	*1793*
Newcastle	3	7	14	16	20	19	12	9	8	9	7
Whitby	7	11	16	20	21	20	21	12	9	10	7
Sunderland	-	-	1	3	7	8	5	5	4	3	3
Stockton	-	-	1	1	2	2	1	1	-	1	1
National	51	96	153	191	248	253	178	126	116	107	87

Source: Fleet lists compiled from local newspapers. PRO, BT 6/94/95; PRO. BT 6/230.
Note: National figures include both England and Scotland.

Table 10. Costs and profitability of *Disko Bay* of Newcastle, 1784-1793

Year	*Expenses (£)*	*Income (£)*	*Profit gained (£)*	*Profit shared (£)*	% [(a)]
1784	1,092	3,025	1,973 [(b)]	1,000	16
1785	2,323	5,003	2,680	1,200	22
1786	2,503	4,876	2,364	1,200	22
1787	2,097	2,742	-	-	-
1788 [(c)]	2,861	2,216	-	-	-
1789	4,039	6,005	1,966	800	11
1790	3,180	4,633	1,453	1,200	19
1791	3,504	5,504	2,000	1,000	15
1792	2,360	2,427	67	-	-
1793	3,071	3,339	268	-	-

Source: Account books of *Disko Bay*, NRO, (Blackett, Wylam).
Notes:
(a) Profit percentage is calculated on the sum shared by the owners and is expressed as a proportion of the fixed and working capital of the vessel.
(b) Profit gained in 1784 was calculated on the inward costs only and included £40-17-11 by a coal voyage to London in 1783.
(c) Costs and income in 1787 and 1788 were run together in the Account Book and have been broken down for the purposes of this table

established interests in the Greenland trade led the way by augmenting the size of their own small fleets. At Newcastle, for example, the principal owners of *Priscilla,* Thomas Frank, William Coulson and William Row, introduced two more ships to the Greenland trade in 1784 and 1785, *Sarah* (300 tons) and *Sarda* (338 tones). They were soon joined by vessels financed by merchants who, hitherto, had no interest in whaling activity. Men such as these financed the emergence of local whaling fleets at Sunderland and Stockton-on-Tees, where their efforts were encouraged by post-war conditions. The release of vessels from the Transport Service provided a pool of sturdy and relatively cheap vessels suitable for employment in the Whale Fishery. At Whitby, for example, several former whalers like *Friendship* and *Adamant,* were re-introduced to the Greenland trade in 1784. The restoration of the bounty payments to £2 per ton in 1782 undoubtedly attracted 'new' owners as well. But as the size of the national whaling fleet increased, the productivity of individual vessels declined. Shipowners experimenting with the whaling trade could hardly have started in more unfavourable circumstances. Whaling was an uncertain and high risk enterprise and for those shipowners who did not know it already, there was plenty of opportunity to learn that lesson, the hard way.

Fitting out and seasonal maintenance costs for a Greenland ship were well in excess of the expenses incurred by shipowners who chose to employ their vessels in other, less hazardous trades. *Aurora* of London, for example, which was valued at £2,000 when she was purchased from the Transport Service in 1784, cost her owners a further £2,771 to outfit for a whaling voyage.[2] A similar amount was paid by William Sparks and Co. of Hull when *Gibraltar* was fitted out there in 1786.[3] Official estimates submitted to the Committee of Trade, also in 1786, considered that £12-12-0 per ton was reasonable for fitting out a second-hand vessel of 200-400 tons.[4] Costs of this order were only taken on in the expectation of high profits. They also encouraged a wider spread of ownership of whaleships than might otherwise have been the case. At Newcastle where twenty vessels sailed from the port in 1787, half of them consisted of ships with six to eight owners, a pattern of ownership which represented only 17 per cent of the total number of ships registered at the port. Clearly, the high fitting-out and maintenance costs together with the substantial risks inherent in the Fishery, physical as well as financial, encouraged a larger spread of ownership. The loss of *Favourite* in 1787, which had twenty owners, undoubtedly had less of an impact than the loss of *Tryall* in 1788 which had only four.

The majority of vessels employed in whaling from Whitby and Newcastle fell into the narrow tonnage range of between 300-350 tons. Typical of these was *Disko Bay,* a vessel for which detailed accounts fortunately survive. *Disko Bay* was a three-masted, ship-rigged vessel of 323 tons built by John Wallis & Co. at South Shields in 1781. In 1784, when she was first introduced to the Greenland trade, she had six principal owners. Two of them, Christopher Blackett and Aubone Surtees, were especially well known in Newcastle mercantile circles. Surtees, particularly, had extensive coal, timber and banking interests. He owned a quarter of *Disko Bay* and was the largest shareholder. Christopher Blackett was a member of a junior branch of the well-known Northumberland landed family and, like Surtees, had extensive business interests in Newcastle. He was, perhaps, best known for his encouragement of George Stephenson's locomotive experiments at Wylam Colliery waggonway in the early nineteenth century. Blackett owned a one-sixth share in *Disko Bay* and kept the accounts of the ship. The remaining owners were John Walker of South Shields, the builder of the ship and Charles Wren, a Newcastle attorney, who also owned a one-sixth share. Richard Lambert a timber and raff merchant and, William Hamilton, the master, both owned a one-eighth part in the vessel.

The decision to employ *Disko Bay* in the Whale Fishery seems to have been influenced by Aubone Surtees' particular interest in whaleships and William Hamilton's considerable experience in the trade.[5] *Disko Bay* was purchased for £3,000 in 1784 and a further £2,073 was expended in outfitting her for the Davis Straits Fishery. Half of the outfitting cost was committed to preparing and equipping the vessel. Doubling and fortifying the hull, whaleboats, specialist cordage, harpoons, lances and the provision of blubber casks represented the bulk of this expense. Victualling costs accounted for 23 per cent of the total and most of the remaining money was committed to port charges, advance wages and incidental expenses disbursed by Captain Hamilton.

Disko Bay's maiden whaling voyage proved to be a successful one. Hamilton brought her back to the Tyne in July 1784 with the produce of four Davis Straits whales which yielded 64 tuns of whale oil and three tons of whalebone. The additional costs of processing this cargo, together with inward pay-bills and insurance premiums amounted to a further £1,092, making a total cost of £3,165 for the initial voyage. *Disko Bay* continued to be employed in the Davis Straits trade until 1793, at first exclusively but later, after 1788, in combination with voyages to the Baltic and in the coal trade.[6] Combining whaling and general trading in the same year remained one of the principal attractions of shipowners employing vessels in the Greenland Fishery. During the rapid expansion of the mid-1780s it was often crucial to the overall annual profitability of their ships, especially those that returned from the Arctic with poor catches.

A combination of over-capacity and falling prices after 1786 proved to be financially disastrous for many shipowners. Almost 40 per cent of the whaling voyages undertaken from the river Tyne in 1787 and 1788 ended in financial loss.[7] National losses in 1788 were estimated to have been almost £200,000.[8] But these losses were not evenly distributed. Shipowners who fitted out their vessels at the beginning of the boom, in 1784 and 1785, and chose to send their vessels to the Davis Straits rather than to the Greenland whaling grounds seem to have stood a better chance of financial survival. Most of the experienced whaler owners at Whitby and Newcastle shifted the emphasis of their efforts from Greenland to the Davis Straits despite the higher costs that this entailed. They were also prepared to tolerate the marginal profitability of their ships, and even loss-making voyages, in the expectation of better returns once national fleet numbers began to decline.

At Whitby in 1785, eleven of the fifteen ships engaged in the whaling trade, over 70 per cent, sailed to Greenland rather than the Davis Straits and there was little difference in the average catch.[9] By 1788, however, the proportion was down to 50 per cent and the Davis Straits ships obtained significantly greater cargoes, almost double those obtained by the Greenland ships. For whaler owners who were new to the trade or merchants financing single ships, the financial consequences of this lower productivity was critical. As a rule of thumb, most whaler owners hoped that their vessels would obtain a cargo of about 60 tuns of whale oil and three tons of whalebone. This would enable them to cover costs. Only one of the Greenland ships at Whitby in 1788, *Two Sisters*, managed to achieve this minimum cargo, whereas six of the Davis Straits ships did so. The financial experience of Nicholas Piper at Whitby serves as a useful case study.[10]

Nicholas Piper was one of a number of merchants and master mariners from the Vale of Pickering who came to be associated with Whitby whaling in the late eighteenth century. William Scoresby was the best known, Crispin Bean was another. Like many of his generation, Nicholas Piper began his career as a master mariner during the 1760s. In 1762 he commanded *Swallow* in the coal and Baltic trades. After 1764 he was the master of *Henrietta* a ship he later came to own. Piper, with others, purchased *Henrietta* in 1775 and entered her into the Greenland trade the following year. By 1783 Piper's ship had already earned profits of £3,000[11] and in four seasons following the end of the American War (1783-86) *Henrietta* secured a further £6,000 profit for her owners. Piper was able to consolidate his position as a shipowner at Whitby and extend his interests at Pickering. He entered a second ship, *Unity*, into the whaling trade in 1785. Built at Scarborough in 1768, she was almost identical in size to *Henrietta*; unfortunately for Piper she did not become a successful whaler. *Unity* secured just 38 butts of blubber, about twelve tuns, on her maiden whaling voyage and her subsequent seasons in the Arctic were little better. Moreover, despite the experience of her master Crispin Bean, *Henrietta* was unable to obtain paying cargoes for several years after 1786. Piper's accounts show no substantial profit payments for the vessel until 1793 (see Table 11).

Table 11. Summary of the accounts of the ship *Henrietta* of Whitby, 251 tons, 1783-1798

Year	Income (£)	Expenses (£)	Profit (£)	Loss (£)	Earnings/ton (£)	Expenses/ton (£)
1783	-	-	750	-	-	-
1784	-	-	2,250	-	-	-
1785	-	-	1,500	-	-	-
1786	-	-	1,500	-	-	-
1787	-	-	-	-	-	-
1788	-	-	-	-	-	-
1789	1,015	1,418	-	403	3.00	5.64
1790	1,180	1,174	6	-	4.69	4.68
1791	1,078	1,089	-	11	4.29	4.33
1792	1,149	1,127	22	-	4.57	4.49
1793	4,421	2,690	1,731	-	17.61	10.75
1794	3,831	3,289	542	-	15.26	13.10
1795	3,478	3,466	12	-	13.85	13.81
1796	5,356	5,084	272	-	21.33	20.25
1797	3.838	2,205	1,633	-	15.29	8.78
1798	4,804	2,446	2,358	-	19.14	9.74

Source: Account books of the *Henrietta* of Whitby, NMM, AMS/35

Piper's experience was probably typical of a majority of owners at Whitby and Newcastle. He decided to persevere with *Henrietta* but not with *Unity* which was withdrawn from the whaling trade after 1788. Of course, there were exceptions to the rule. At Howdon-on-Tyne one of Samuel Hurry's whalers, *Jason*, earned profits of between £1,200-£1,500 for each of its whaling voyages between 1786 and 1788. Given that a vessel like *Jason* (243 tons) might have been expected to earn about £80[12] for a London coal voyage, this ship earned as much during a four-month Greenland voyage as she might normally have earned over two years in the coal trade. Most of the shipowners who participated in the whaling trade looked for profits of this order, but few experienced them. At the other end of the scale there were some unmitigated financial disasters. The owners of the Newcastle ships *Minerva* and *Eclipse* collectively lost almost £5,000 on the voyages of their ships in 1787 and 1788, and the combined loss of the Newcastle whaling fleet amounted to £10,000.[13] The burden fell most heavily on those who engaged single ships and had little background in the trade. These were the shipowners who withdrew from the trade as quickly as they had entered it. Not surprisingly, the size of the local whaling fleet fell rapidly after 1788. By 1793 it was down to eighteen ships and the outbreak of the French War reduced it even further.

As if to compound the problems already being experienced, the whaling season of 1792 was a disastrous one. There were a number of shipwrecks, including *Kitty* of Newcastle and *Harpooner* of Whitby, and many of the surviving ships returned damaged and with poor catches. Four of the Tyne whalers were 'clean', the other four caught only seven whales between them. At Whitby four ships returned 'clean' and the remaining two ships caught a single whale each.

On Tyneside the owners of one of the veteran Greenland ships, *Priscilla*, decided to try their luck with a voyage to the Southern Whale Fishery in 1792-93.[14] It was the first of only a handful of voyages undertaken by vessels based in north-east England between 1792-1850. It was also something of a collaborative effort between owners at Newcastle and Whitby. The master of *Priscilla* in 1792-93 was Cuthbert Richardson, whose company had financed some whaling voyages to the Davis Straits from Whitby between 1784-89. Richardson took *Priscilla* to the Pacific coast of South America on a voyage that lasted eighteen months. *Priscilla* returned to the Tyne in September 1793 with the produce of 35 sperm whales and several thousand seal skins.[15] The average cargo of oil obtained by British whalers in the Southern Whale Fishery at this date amounted to 114 tuns of oil representing a value of £4,307 per vessel.[16] *Priscilla* appears to have achieved this average cargo and perhaps slightly more. The additional income derived from the sale of 5,000 seal skins *Priscilla* is reported to have obtained, probably pushed her total earnings to almost £5,000, substantially more than the earnings of the Greenland ships. If the owners of *Priscilla* hoped to repeat the experience they did not get the chance to do so; *Priscilla* was captured by a French privateer off the North Cape in 1794 and sold as a prize.

The outbreak of the French Wars presented new opportunities, particularly for the employment of ships in the Transport Service, and many former whalers were engaged by the government. At Newcastle a single ship, *John and Margaret*, sailed from the port between 1794 and 1796. Whitby, however, continued to send four ships to the Arctic including the veterans *Henrietta* and *Volunteer*. The success of these vessels is outlined in Table 12. With fewer ships on the whaling grounds the chances of success for those that remained improved considerably. Under the command of William Scoresby Snr. *Henrietta* moved back into profit (see Table 11). On Tyneside the owners of *John and Margaret* benefited from a significant improvement in the earnings of that ship between 1794 and 1798.

Table 12. Comparative performance of whalers at Newcastle and Whitby, 1793-98

Year	No. of vessels	Tonnage	Blubber (tun)	Bone (ton)	Oil value (£)	Bone value (£)	Total value (£)
Whitby							
1793	7	2,133	497	16.50	11,431	3,300	14,731
1794	6	1,760	728	29.50	18,928	3,835	22,763
1795	4	1,139	463	15.25	14,353	2,592	16,945
1796	4	1,139	528	20.75	17,424	2,448	19,872
1797	4	1,139	647	23.50	20,704	1,880	22,584
1798	4	1,139	317	10.60	9,193	742	9,935
Newcastle							
1793	7	2,302	456	18.80	10,488	3,760	14,248
1794	1	397	173	8.20	4,498	1,066	5,564
1795	1	397	122	5.90	3,782	1,003	4,785
1796	1	397	184	8.80	6,072	1,038	7,110
1797	2	697	314	13.75	10,048	1,100	11,148
1798	3	1,008	372	18.30	10,788	1,281	12,069

Source: PRO, ZHC 1/772. Accounts relating to the Whale Fisheries, BPP, 1823
PRO, BT6/230, fol. 95. See Jackson, G. Whaling Trade, Appendix 8.

The experience of whaler owners at Whitby and Newcastle between 1783 and 1798 reflected the experience of whaler owners nationally. They responded to the effects of over-fishing, over-capacity, governmental policy and war by withdrawing ships, deploying the remaining vessels more flexibly and accepting lower profits. Elsewhere vessels owned at Sunderland and Stockton-on-Tees were also engaged in whaling activity between 1785 and 1798. There were strong connections between these ports and in some cases shipowners appear to have integrated their whaling effort. The connections between Sunderland and Whitby and, between Whitby and Stockton-on-Tees, were particularly strong even though their direct involvement in the Greenland trade was relatively short lived.

Stockton-on-Tees 1785-1792

Stockton-on-Tees was a relatively small port at the end of the eighteenth century. Only 47 vessels were registered there in 1795[17] most of them sloops and brigs sailing in the coasting trade. There was a small export trade to northern Europe and Stockton owned vessels occasionally sailed further afield, into the Mediterranean or across the Atlantic to America and the West Indies. During the American War of Independence, for example, *Amphitrite* (350 tons) and *Preston* (300 tons), sailed from London to New York with provisions for General Howe's beleaguered army. The owners of both took the precaution of obtaining Letters of Marque for their voyages into the American war zone.[18] But large vessels like *Amphitrite* and *Preston* rarely sailed directly from Stockton even though ships of a similar size were regularly built there. The Tees was a shallow and inconvenient river at the end of the eighteenth century. Its meandering course was strewn with sandbanks and even small vessels had difficulty in navigating it. Incoming ships could take several days to reach Stockton from Teesmouth and their cargoes were often transferred into lighters or landed onshore at Newport or Cargo Fleet on the way. In November 1775, Robert Richmond, the exasperated master of *Betsy*, a local sloop of 70 tons, was forced to anchor for a week in the estuary because of '*the tides flowing out too late and too soon for going any higher up till Saturday next*'.[19]

The principal imports at Stockton, flax, hemp, iron and timber reflected, amongst other things, the growing importance of shipbuilding at the port. Stockton built vessels could be found almost anywhere, sailing in almost any trade: *Experiment*, built in 1798, was an East Indiaman of over 500 tons; *Fox* was a 55 ton sloop built for the owners of Boulby Alum Works;[20] *Sunderland*, 197 tons, and *Grenville Bay*, 320 tons, were employed as Greenland whalers from the Wear and the Tyne.

Stockton itself had little connection with Arctic whaling before 1786. There were few vessels suited to the task and a limited market into which they could sell. Nevertheless, the peculiar economic and commercial circumstances prevailing in the shipping industry at the end of the American War attracted a number of local shipowners to try their luck in the Greenland trade. The first whaler to sail directly from Stockton-on-Tees was *Loyalty*, a brig built at Whitby in 1772. She had eight owners in 1786 and was regularly engaged in the coal and Baltic trades prior to her use as a whaling ship. *Loyalty* sailed as part of the Whitby fleet in 1785-86, an indication, perhaps, of the lack of adequate facilities then available at Stockton. By 1788, however, there was a whale oil yard and warehouse at Portrack and *Loyalty* delivered her cargoes of bone and blubber directly to it. In 1787-88 *Loyalty* was joined by a second Greenland ship, *Collins*, Dutch built and captured as a prize during the American War. It turned out to be an unsuccessful and short-lived partnership. *Collins* fitted out and sailed from Liverpool in 1787 returning to Stockton in July with the blubber of two whales. But her voyage from the Tees the following year was unsuccessful and the ship returned 'clean'. *Collins* sailed again from Liverpool in 1789 and was withdrawn from the Greenland trade on her return.[21] *Loyalty* was much more successful obtaining fourteen whales in four

Table 13. Earnings of *Loyalty* of Stockton-on-Tees, 1786-1789

Year	*Catch (whales)*	*Oil (tuns)*	*Bone (cwt.)*	*Total value (£)*	*Earnings/ton (£)*	*Profit (£)*	*Loss (£)*
1786	4	35	24	1,439	6.5	-	1,153
1787	2	40	21	1,352	6.2	272	-
1788	2	25	18	1,098	5.0	18	-
1789	6	45	42	1,463	6.5	383	-

Source: Primage Account Books, Stockton receipts, TWAD, GU/TH/221.
Note: A quantity of seals is included in the total value in 1787 and 1788.

voyages between 1786 and 1789. Additional earnings in the coal and Baltic trades boosted profitability and helped to sustain her employment as a whaler. After an absence of two years, *Loyalty* sailed to the Davis Straits in 1792-93. In 1792 when several whalers were wrecked and many others returned damaged and 'clean', *Loyalty* captured two large whales which produced 28 tuns of oil and almost 1½ tons of whalebone. The cargo was worth over £1,000 and the voyage of 1793 earned a similar amount. *Loyalty* was then withdrawn from whaling activity altogether. In November 1793, on her arrival in the Tees from a Baltic voyage, *Loyalty* was advertised for sale:

> *'TO BE SOLD by auction at Robert Coats, the GREEN DRAGON on Wed. 1 January 1794–the brigantine* Loyalty *of Stockton (Robert Jackson, master) lying at Portrack near Stockton. She is a square-sterned vessel of about 216 tons burden, carries 16 keels of coals, is remarkably well-found, has a complete set of boats, casks, whale-lines…utensils and instruments for the Greenland Whale Fishery…is doubled etc.*
>
> *A purchaser wishing to continue the vessel in the Fishery may have a convenient boiling house, with good warehouses for stores, oil etc. at Portrack at a lower rent than most of the ports in the north of England.'*[22]

Loyalty returned to general trade. She was reported at The Sound in July 1794, on passage from Stockton to St. Petersburg in ballast. *Loyalty* was eventually captured by a French privateer off Brest on passage from London to Oporto in 1796.

Whaling from Stockton-on-Tees had little economic importance for the port, but it turned out to have considerable legal significance for the Greenland Fishery in general. In December 1786, the master of *Loyalty* appeared as the defendant in a case brought by the owners of *Success* of London. They sought compensation for a valuable whale which was killed but later lost by the harpooners of *Success*. The whale was subsequently recovered and flensed by the crew of *Loyalty*. Since it had long been the custom among Greenland whalers that the carcass of an abandoned whale became the property of the ship that discovered it:

> *'to the entire satisfaction of the court they found for the defendant with costs...by which verdict a new question of the utmost importance for the Greenland Trade is settled.'* [23]

A rare survival amongst the records of *Loyalty*, are the registration documents relating to the whaleboats carried by the ship. The Greenland trade was heavily regulated by government and shipowners were obliged to ensure the suitability of all equipment carried by their vessels. This included a requirement to licence each of the whaleboats. Despite her size *Loyalty* carried six substantial whaleboats ranging in length from the 27'5" of whaleboats one and two, to the 24' whaleboats five and six. Each whaleboat was propelled by six oars. Detailed descriptions of their construction provide maritime historians with a rare insight into these famous small boats.[24]

The direct participation of Stockton vessels in the whaling trade lasted for only seven years, but the experience of shipowners at the port was, in many ways, typical of a general response to the difficulties and financial implications of Arctic whaling enterprise in this period. Whaling at Stockton was an irrelevance to the long-term growth and development of the port although there were a number of subsequent indirect associations with it. One of the most interesting was the employment of a Stockton-on-Tees registered brig, *Calypso*, as part of the Tyne whaling fleet between 1805-1808. Built at Hylton Ferry on the river Wear in 1796 and subsequently transferred from Stockton to Newcastle, *Calypso*'s career as a whaler was short-lived. She spent the majority of her working life as a collier, just as the majority of other Stockton vessels did. Elsewhere, Stockton-built vessels developed long-established links with the whaling trade,[25] which endured down to recent times. The last commercial whalers on the British register, *Southern Harvester* and *Southern Venturer*, sold to the Japanese between 1961-1963 were built on the Tees at Haverton Hill, only a few miles downstream from the site of a former whale oil yard at Portrack.

Sunderland, 1785-1798

Sunderland, after Newcastle-upon-Tyne, was the most substantial port of north-east England. In 1800 it was the fourth ranking port in the Kingdom, by registered tonnage, after Liverpool, Newcastle and Hull. At the beginning of the eighteenth century Sunderland harbour was choked with sandbanks and notoriously difficult to navigate but systematic harbour improvement by the River Wear Improvement Commission contributed to the rapid development of the port. By the end of the century there were piers and lighthouses at the harbour entrance and most of the sandbanks were gone.[26]

Sunderland shipping reflected the demands of the coal trade which dominated the activity of the port. The bulk of Sunderland's foreign trade was with northern Europe and the Baltic with a smaller proportion of vessels engaged in southern European and transatlantic trading.

Although the patterns of trade at Newcastle and Sunderland were virtually identical, the patterns of ownership were significantly different. The most striking characteristic of Sunderland shipowning in 1786 was the predominance of single and double ownership which represented 56 and 26 per cent respectively, of the total number of vessels registered at the port.[27] At Newcastle these categories of ownership represented just 18 and 13 per cent. The average size of vessels at Sunderland in 1786 was 140 tons. Since, as a general rule, smaller vessels had fewer owners, this may explain the infrequency of multiple ownership. The Sunderland whalers were, however, much larger than the average size of vessels owned on the Wear and their ownership patterns differed significantly from the norm. Six of the eight vessels used as whalers at Sunderland in 1788 had between six and thirteen owners, a pattern of ownership which was not typical of the port. The costs incurred and the risks inherent in the Greenland trade clearly encouraged a wider spread of ownership. Only one of the Sunderland whalers in 1788 had less than three owners, *Jenny's Adventure*, 163 tons, owned by Thomas Weatherall, a brazier, and William Friend, an ironmonger.[28] Neither of these men appear to have had interests in other vessels at Sunderland in 1786 although the vessel was employed as a whaler at Whitby before that date. By contrast, the owners of *Leviathan*, Ralph Marshall and James Robinson were amongst the principal shipowners on the Wear in 1786. Both men had an interest in two other Sunderland whalers, *Blackett* and *Horn*.[29] Some ships intended for the Whale Fishery were re-registered to incorporate multiple ownership. When *Urania*, 163 tons, was first registered at Sunderland in 1786 she had two owners, George Matthews, a master mariner and Robert Hutton, a coal fitter. In 1788 after a major refit, *Urania* was re-registered with eight owners; Matthews and Hutton continued their interests in the vessel.[30] Similarly, *Sunderland*, 197 tons, which had one owner in 1786, Ann Havelock, a widow and seven owners in 1787, was registered with thirteen owners after fitting out for a whaling voyage.[31] With one or two notable exceptions the majority of owners at Sunderland appear to have had little or no connection with Arctic whaling before 1786. Only Kenneth Thompson,

Cove of South Shields, whaling in Baffin Bay, c.1830.

George Palmer Collection.

Courtesy of Stephen Wolfenden.

Sarah of North Shields whaling in the Davis Straits, c.1784. *John Askew.*

This superb whaling composition probably depicts a scene from **Sarah's** maiden whaling voyage in 1784 and seems to have been commissioned by her captain and part owner, Thomas Frank Jnr. (1754–1807).

Courtesy of Christopher Foley.

Greenland Right Whale. Sustained a European whaling industry for three hundred years. It was exploited to the point of extinction by the whalermen and became the first of the great whales to gain protection from the International Whaling Commission.

Carr Rock and pier, Spittal. Once the only deep water anchorage in the river Tweed. It was used as a mooring place for the Berwick whalers between 1807 and 1837. The derelict industrial buildings in the background stand on the site of a former whale oil manufactory.

THE INHABITANTS

OF

NORTH SHIELDS.

A HAND BILL having appeared, calling a Meeting of the Inhabitants of the Townships of North Shields and Tynemouth, on Thursday the 21st Instant (To-morrow) for the purpose of taking into consideration the propriety of forming a GAS COMPANY, for lighting the Houses and Shops within those Townships; the Tradesmen and Inhabitants at large, are entreated to PAUSE before they commit themselves, by giving their Sanction to such a Measure, and to direct their Attention to the following FACTS, which are submitted for their consideration.

It is well known to you all, that there are five Ships fitted out for the Greenland and Davis' Straights Fisheries in this Port, each of which, on an average, expends in Wages, Provisions, &c. £3,000 upon this Voyage alone, four-fifths of which are expended in North Shields. It may not be so generally known, although it is no less true, that the Masters, Officers, and Seamen resident in this Town, and who are employed in Ships belonging to other Ports, in the Whale Fishery, amount to upwards of 500, each of whom, on an average, earns upon the Voyage £25, four-fifths of which may also be calculated to be put into circulation in the Town,—over and above the benefit which thus arises to the Inhabitants of the Town, ought to be taken into the Account, the National Bounty received by each Ship, and the Profit derived from the introduction of the Oil into the Country (every Ton of which is actually so much increase to the Wealth of the Kingdom) both of which are likewise expended, or applied in Commercial Pursuits in North Shields. To say nothing of the Support to which the Adventurer in so hazardous an undertaking is intitled, the summary detail above offered to your Notice, contains Arguments sufficiently cogent, to induce every reflecting Mind to give the most vigorous Support to the Whale Fishery, and to resist any innovation that may have a tendency, however remote, to weaken or depress the ardour of the Adventurer.

With the evident advantages which result to the Public from the Whale Fishery, let us briefly contrast the Scheme of a Gas Company; the sole object of which, as may be collected from the Hand Bill, circulated by the Projectors, is their own " *Profit.*"

It is sufficiently ascertained in a neighbouring Town, possessing manifold advantages over this Place for the supply of Gas at a moderate rate, that the Expence to Individuals of lighting with Gas, is equal to that attending the Use of Whale Oil, so that the Gas has not even cheapness to give it a preference to the Oil; and it appears to be a difficult Task to adduce any Argument or Reason why the PUBLIC of North Shields should give their Countenance and Support to the introduction of a Novelty, which, whilst it can yield them no solid Advantage, has a direct tendency to stop the source from whence a great Portion of their prosperity flows.—The superior brilliancy of the Light afforded by the Gas, will no doubt be pressed as a sufficient reason for its adoption!—but even this is more than counter-balanced by the noxious and unwholesome stench produced by it: and is not the Light from the Oil Lamps sufficiently vivid for every Purpose of the Tradesman?

Much more might be added on the Subject, which the Limits of a Hand Bill will not admit; but to those who look forward to Consequences, and attentively scan Causes and their Effects, enough, it is hoped, has been urged to secure their strenuous co-operation to crush so impolitic a Measure in its rise.

A newspaper advertisement urging the inhabitants of North Shields to consider the consequences of coal gas for the whaling industry *c.1820*

Lord Gambier, photographed at Kirkcaldy in 1860.

Built at Monkwearmouth in 1826 and employed as a whaler from the river Tyne between 1831-1844. **Lord Gambier**, (Cpt. Richard Warham), was associated with the rediscovery of Cumberland Sound in 1840-41 and the search for the Franklin Expedition in 1847-48. She was wrecked in Baffin Bay in 1862.

Fife Council Museums: Kirkcaldy Museums and Art Galleries.

John Patterson (1805-1879), last of the old whaler captains of North East England. He sailed fifty years to the Arctic whaling grounds between 1814-1863.

Courtesy of John Milward.

Robert Boston (1822-1891), of Spittal near Berwick, who served several voyages as a cooper's mate aboard **Lady Jane** during the 1840s.

James Williamson (1814-1899). Surgeon of the **Lady Jane** 1835-37. His journal of the ice-drift voyage of 1835-36 provides a graphic account of the experiences of the crew. Williamson subsequently spent many years as a doctor in South Shields. He died in London in 1899.

William Jackson (1814-1902). Jackson served as a boatsteerer in the **Norfolk** of Berwick during her ice-drift voyage of 1836-37 and was the last survivor of her unfortunate crew. He died at the grand old age of 88.

Resolution of Whitby. *Thomas Buttersworth, Sr.*

Built by Fishburn and Broderick for William Scoresby in 1802-1803. Scoresby is reputed to have commissioned the painting for the stern cabin of **Fame**, hence its rather unusual shape. **Resolution** was sold to owners at Peterhead in 1829 and wrecked in Baffin Bay the following year.

The Kendall Whaling Museum, Sharon, Massachusetts, USA.

Whalers off the Tyne, c.1835. *Attributed to J.W. Carmichael.*

The vessel in the foreground carries a blue pennant at the masthead with the initials GB, for **Grenville Bay**. She was built at Stockton-on-Tees in 1783. The other whaler is probably **Lord Gambier**.

Torre Abbey museum and Gallery.

Table 14. Performance of Sunderland vessels, 1793-98

Year	*No. of vessels*	*Tonnage*	*Blubber (tuns)*	*Bone (tons)*	*Oil value (£)*	*Bone value (£)*	*Total (£)*
1793	3	850	232	10.50	5,336	2,100	7,436
1794	2	450	178	7.25	4,628	942	5,570
1795	1	253	84	3.50	2,604	595	3,199
1796	1	253	141	6.00	4,653	708	5,361
1797	2	587	243	11.25	7,776	900	8,676
1798	2	587	206	9.50	5,974	665	6,639

Source: PRO, ZHC 1/772, Accounts Relating to the Whale Fisheries, BPP, 1823.
PRO, BT 6/230, fol. 95. See Jackson, G. Whaling Trade, Appendix 8.

principal owner of *Queen*, 316 tons, together with John and Robert Barry, had extensive experience of the Greenland trade at other ports. Thompson commanded the Tyne whaler *John and Margaret* between 1776-1786 and the Barry brothers acquired their whaling skills at Whitby.[32] They represented another manifestation of the connection between Whitby and Sunderland which had endured since the 1750s. The master of Whitby's first whaler, *Sea Nymph*, came from Sunderland; the masters of Sunderland's last whalers, *Ariel* and *Hunter*, came from Robin Hood's Bay.

Sunderland's direct involvement in Arctic whaling began in 1774 when *Hazard* sailed from the Wear for the first time. She was withdrawn after three voyages. Sunderland resumed its connection with Arctic enterprise in 1785 when *Blackett* sailed to the whaling grounds. Eventually ten vessels were employed as whalers from the river Wear between 1785 and 1798. Most of them sailed to the Greenland Fishery and despite difficult economic circumstances some realised a profit on their voyages. In 1787, *Grampus* earned a profit of £900 and two other ships *Jenny's Adventure* and *Sunderland* appear to have made successful voyages as well. By contrast, the owners of *Queen* sustained a substantial loss and withdrew the ship from the Greenland trade in 1788. It made more sense to engage the ship in voyages to Virginia and the West Indies where the prospect of profit was more assured. The owners of *Urania* lost more than £1,000 in 1788 and did not recover their investment before the ship was wrecked off the east coast of Greenland in 1790 with 2,000 seals on board but no whales. The insurance value of *Urania* and its cargo was considerably less than the cumulative investment they had made in the ship.

The owners of *Leviathan* were more fortunate. In 1789 the ship suffered major structural damage on the whaling grounds and arrived in the Wear in a shattered condition:

> '*The* Leviathan, *Barry, arrived at Sunderland from Greenland with two fish and four unicorns.*[33] *She was struck by a field of ice which obliged her to leave the country and was with much difficulty brought home, having a large hole in her bottom when she came into port which was covered with old sails, oakum etc.*'[34]

In 1792 all of the Sunderland whalers returned 'clean' and one of them, *Horn*, was sold to London owners after her return from the Davis Straits the following year.[35] Thereafter, between 1793 and 1798, only one or two vessels per season were sent to the whaling grounds. The owners of *Sunderland* persevered until 1795 when the ship was captured by a French privateer off Shetland. In 1796 *Hunter* earned £5,361 for a Davis Straits voyage and became the most successful ship then operating from the region. A second vessel, *Ariel*, commenced whaling activity from the Wear in 1797, but was withdrawn the following year. *Ariel* and *Hunter* with their whaling equipment, the lease on the whale oil yard at Hylton together with various wharves and warehouses at Monkwearmouth Shore were advertised for sale in 1798. Both vessels were sold into the Hull whaling fleet and many Wearside whalermen moved with them. In 1795 all of the harpooners mustered to *Enterprise* at Hull, seven in total, came from Sunderland.[36] John and Robert Barry left whaling altogether to develop their interests in general trade. They succeeded in establishing a family shipowning interest at Sunderland which survived for much of the nineteenth century. Robert Barry died at Sunderland in 1822 and his brother John died there in 1840. Ironically, they abandoned the Greenland trade just as the shipowners at Newcastle and Whitby renewed their interests in it.

References

1. Jackson, G. *The British Whaling Trade*, Appendix 6.

2. Cost of the ship *Aurora* in the year 1784, PRO, BT 6/93.

3. Jackson, G. *Hull in the Eighteenth Century* (Oxford University Press, 1972), p. 169.

4. Public Record Office (PRO), BT 6/93. folio 219.

5. Hamilton served in various capacities, including harpooner and master, on whaling ships sailing from Whitby between 1767-1779.

6. Barrow, T, 'The Account Books of the *Disko Bay* of Newcastle 1784-1802: A Case Study of Vessel Management, Utilisation and Profitability in the British Shipping Industry' in *Mariner's Mirror*, Vol.81, 2, 1995.

7. Barrow, A. 'North East Coast Whale Fishery, 1750-1850', University of Northumbria, Ph.D, (1989).

8. PRO, BT 6/94, folios 87-91.

9. The Greenland ships secured an average cargo of 118 butts of blubber, the Davis Straits ships, 121 butts. The most successful of the Whitby whalers in 1785, *Henrietta*, with 185 butts of blubber, had sailed to Greenland. *Source:* An Account of Primage duty received for the Trinity House at Newcastle, 5 January 1785–5 January 1786, Tyne Wear Archives Dept. (TWAD), GU/TH/221.

10. Piper, like Scoresby, came from a farming background. Several branches of the family had been freeholders in and around Pickering since the sixteenth century. The elder Nicholas Piper is credited with the construction of a large house in Pickering Market Place. He died about 1820. See Clitheroe, G. *The Ancient Mariners of Pickering* (Beck Isle Museum, 1976). I am indebted to Peter Barton for drawing my attention to this valuable, if somewhat obscure, publication.

11. Account books of the ship *Henrietta* of Whitby, National Maritime Museum (NMM), AMS/35.

12. Coal Trade Tracts, 1787, (British Library), 8244.

13. Barrow, A. 'Whale Fishery', University of Northumbria, Ph.D, (1989), Table 18.2, p.121.

14. The Southern or Sperm Whale Fishery was developed in England by American whalermen who, as Empire Loyalists, left the American colonies at the outbreak of the War of Independence in 1775. Chief amongst them was Samuel Enderby of Boston and Alexander Champion. In the early years, the whaling grounds were generally confined to the mid-Atlantic, between Cape Verde and the coast of Brazil, in latitudes 31-36°S. By the 1790s the Southern Fishery had been extended into the Pacific and Indian Oceans. Whalers engaged in the Southern Fishery, usually smaller than their Northern Fishery

counterparts, remained at sea longer (two to three years in most cases), and rendered their oil in try-works on board ship. British involvement in the Southern Whale Fishery was dominated by London merchants, but ships from other ports undertook occasional voyages. There were three recorded voyages from North-East ports between 1792-1845. In 1792-93, *Priscilla* sailed to the Pacific coast of South America. In 1802, *Edwinstow* sailed to the same region from the Tyne but was detained by the Spanish at La Concepción, Chile, in February 1804 and sold as a prize. Finally, in 1845, the Newcastle registered *Mohawk*, 234 tons, was equipped and provisioned at Berwick. No further detail relating to the duration or success of this voyage has been found. British whalers sailed to the Southern Fishery until 1850 but the trade was dominated by American ships and immortalised by Melville in *Moby Dick*.

15. *Newcastle Courant*, 14 September 1793.

16. Jackson, G. *Whaling Trade*, Table 8, p.112.

17. 1795 is the first date for which evidence is available. See Brewster, J. *The Parochial History and Antiquities of Stockton on Tees, 1796* (reprinted 1971 by Patrick and Shotton).

18. PRO, HCA 26/64.

19. Barton, P. *The Trade of the Tees in the Eighteenth Century*, Lecture notes, 17-18 October 1970.

20. Barton, P. Lecture notes.

21. Barrow, A. 'Whale Fishery', University of Northumbria, Ph.D. (1989). Chap.6, p.139.

22. *Newcastle Chronicle*, November-December 1793.

23. *Newcastle Chronicle*, 23 December 1786.

24. Copy of licences for whaleboats belonging to the ship *Loyalty* of Stockton-on-Tees, (PRO, CUST. 89/154). I am grateful to Peter Barton for this reference and for the information in footnote 25 below.

25. The earliest was *Gibraltar* (ex-*Ranger*) built at Stockton in 1753 and whaling from Dartmouth, 1777-81; others include *Grenville Bay*, built 1783 and whaling from Newcastle, 1816-40, and several Scottish whalers, *Caledonia* of Kirkaldy (1816), *Hercules* of Aberdeen (1781) and *Enterprise* of Peterhead (1844).

26. Miller, S. 'The River Wear Commission, 1717-1854', *Antiquities of Sunderland* (Sunderland Antiquarian Society), XXVII, (1977-79).

27. Customs Port Shipping Registers, Sunderland, TWAD, Ex/Sul/1.

28. Ex/Sul/1, No. 25, 1787.

29. Ex/Sul/1, No. 335, 1786; No. 21, 1787; No. 7, 1787.

30. Ex/Sul/1, No. 270, 1786 and No. 12, 1788.

31. Ex/Sul/1, No. 166, 1786 and No. 29, 1787.

32. John Barry began his whaling career as an apprentice on *Volunteer* in 1775 and progressed to the position of harpooner of *Nautilus* by 1785. Robert Barry, also served on board various Whitby whalers between 1776-1786, including *Delight* (1776-77) and *Addison* (1782-85). The oldest brother, William Barry, was a young apprentice on *Volunteer* during the voyage of 1772 and served in the ship throughout the 1770s. See Whitby Muster rolls, Whitby Literary and Philosophical Society (WLPS), *Volunteer*, No. 21, 1773; No. 244, 1775; No. 123, 1777; *Nautilus*, No. 282, 1785; *Delight*, No. 56, 1776; and *Addison*, No. 84, 1783.

33. The whalermen commonly referred to narwhals as unicorns.

34. *Newcastle Advertiser*, 25 July 1789.

35. *Horn* had a long and distinguished whaling career at Dundee between 1806 and 1852. She was wrecked near St. Andrews with a full cargo of blubber and bone in November 1852 after completing over 50 voyages to the Arctic.

36. Muster rolls of *Enterprise*, Hull Trinity House (HTH), p.132, No. 19, 1795.

4

'A new era in the Whale Fishery [when] the success of former times has been surpassed'

[Young, G. *History of Whitby*, 1817]

War and Peace, 1798-1820

The Northern Whale Fishery entered a golden age during the early years of the French Wars. For two decades after 1798 the size of catches and the levels of profit derived from them regularly exceeded anything that had been achieved in earlier years. Nationally, the tonnage of vessels employed in Arctic whaling between 1790 and 1800 was halved from 30,819 tons to 15,405 tons.[1] At the same time productivity amongst the remaining ships improved dramatically. At Whitby for example the average seasonal catch per ship between 1803 and 1812 was 12.5 whales, more than three times as much as it had been during the 1780s. In 1811, seven ships caught 171 whales and in 1814, *Resolution*, Captain Kearsley, secured 28 whales yielding 230 tuns of whale oil: '*...the largest quantity ever imported into Whitby in any one ship and probably the greatest quantity ever brought from Greenland by any ship of a like burden.*'[2]

Resolution was purpose-built for the Whale Fishery by Fishburn and Broderick at a cost of £7,791. She sailed to Greenland for the first time in 1803 and subsequently, under the command of the Scoresbys, father and son, became the most successful ship in the Whitby whaling fleet. According to George Young: '*In 10 successive voyages, beginning in 1803, the* Resolution, *Scoresby, obtained no less than 249 whales, yielding 2,034 tuns of oil.*'[3]

The personal roles of the Scoresbys was crucial to the success of *Resolution* and contributed significantly to the consolidation of whaling at Whitby. At a time when the older, Greenland whaling grounds, were showing signs of over-fishing, Scoresby appreciated the need for further exploration and a search for new stocks of whales. In 1806 in the Greenland Sea west of Spitzbergen, he took *Resolution* to 81°30' N, the most northerly point ever achieved by a sailing ship at that date and just 500 miles from the North Pole.[4] William Scoresby's consistent success as a whale hunter became legendary. Other captains often followed him in the expectation of finding whales themselves. In 30 voyages between 1793-1823, first as master of *Henrietta*, subsequently of *Resolution* and other ships, William Scoresby, Snr., is said to have made a profit of £90,000 for himself and the owners.[5]

The overall profit of *Henrietta*, alone, was calculated at £53,553-18s-3d '*being upwards of 1,600 per cent on the whole of the first cost of the adventure*'.[6] Was *Henrietta* a typical whaler, or were her profits exceptional? Comparisons with other Whitby ships, such as *Volunteer*, *Lively*, *Aimwell* and *Experiment* between 1805-1812, reveal that *Henrietta* was a highly successful Greenlandman. Whereas the average catch of the Whitby fleet during these years was 1,037 tuns of oil; *Henrietta* secured 1,209 tuns at an average of 151 tuns per season. *Resolution* with a total catch of 1,679 tuns, was undoubtedly the most successful ship.[7]

On Tyneside where the Greenland fleet had contracted to a single vessel, *John and Margaret*, between 1794-1796, the rising productivity of the national whaling fleet soon encouraged a revival of interest. Despite a fluctuation in the number of whaling ships operating from the river Tyne between 1790-1807, Newcastle's share of the national trade increased from an average of 5 per cent of national whale oil imports in 1790-1792 to 9 per cent between 1805-1807. Similarly her share of the whalebone trade increased from just over 9 per cent in 1790-1792 to just over 13 per cent between 1805-1807.[8]

The revival began in 1797 when *Sarah* resumed her career as a whaling ship. *Mars* and *John and Margaret* had also been used as Greenland ships in the earlier period and *Lady Jane* sailed from the river Tyne for the first time in 1804. She had originally been employed from Hull. The number of whaling ships sailing from Newcastle peaked at twelve in 1803 before falling back to an average of eight per year between 1804 and 1810. Several of these ships revealed a noticeable change in patterns of ownership compared to previous years. Whereas many of the vessels used as whalers during the expansion of the 1780s had been owned by generalshipowners with no special interest in the processing and distribution of whale products, a significant number of the vessels employed after 1795 were operated by specialist merchants. Hull, which came to dominate British whaling after 1800, led the way in this development. Wealthy oil merchants and shipowners like Eggington & Co. and William Lee & Co. were prepared to invest as much as £10,000 in acquiring, fitting-out and maintaining a whaling ship in the Greenland trade. Some of these firms at Hull soon came to operate small fleets of whalers.

At Newcastle the trend towards a greater concentration of whaling ships in the hands of fewer owners was particularly noticeable. Between 1800 and 1810, two families of shipowners and oil merchants came to dominate the Greenland trade on Tyneside; Edward and Thomas Hurry of Howdonpans, and John and James Humble of Felling Shore. Collectively, they owned seven of the ten whalers operating from the river Tyne in 1804. The Hurry family had long established interests in Greenland whaling which they originally developed in conjunction with a prosperous shipbuilding enterprise after 1758. They persevered with Arctic whaling during the years of contraction after 1790, and responded to the increased productivity of their veteran whaler, *John and Margaret*, by sending additional ships to the whaling grounds; *Prescott* in 1802, *Norfolk* in 1803 and *Howe* in 1804. This small fleet of vessels may have represented a last desperate gamble to stave off business failure. The collapse of the shipbuilding business and the subsequent bankruptcy of Francis, Thomas and Edward Hurry, forced the sale of their Greenland ships in 1805-1806. Three were sold locally and continued to be used as whalers from the river Tyne. The fourth vessel, *Prescott*, was sold to William Lee & Co., whaler owners of Hull, and used from that port until 1822.[9]

The bankruptcy of the Hurry shipyard at Howdon had two principal causes; over-capitalization and a decline in the number of orders received from the Admiralty after the Peace of Amiens in 1802.[10] A third and equally important cause, was over-investment in Greenland whaling. Even in a period of rising profitability, the initial costs of outfitting and provisioning a Greenland ship were difficult to recover in a single voyage. Although they already owned the vessels committed to whaling after 1802, only *John and Margaret* had a favourable account book and the earnings of that ship were affected by the death of its experienced Greenland captain, Jacob Jameson, during the 1802 voyage. In 1803, under a new master, Ralph Crawford, *John and Margaret* captured only two whales. The other ships, *Prescott* and *Norfolk*, caught three each. These cargoes are unlikely to have realised a profit, and their voyages in 1804 were little better. Collectively they represented a loss of at least £8,000-£10,000, a considerable sum even in a period of rapid inflation.[11] These losses, compounded with the difficulties of the shipbuilding business, tipped the scales and precipitated the bankruptcy. The assets of the Hurry family, including their whaling ships, were sold off and a 40-year connection with the Greenland trade came to an end. The veteran *John and Margaret*, built in Massachusetts as far back as 1736, soldiered on under new owners for a few more years. But in 1808, after 42 consecutive voyages to the Arctic, she was sold and broken up.

The other principal whaler owners on the Tyne between 1800 and 1811 were John and James Humble. They owned a whale oil yard and warehouses at Felling Shore, as well as substantial interests in the Felling Brewery. Their first vessel, *Middleton*, entered the whaling trade in 1801; a second, *Isabella*, in 1802, and a third, *Katherine*,[12] in 1804. *Middleton* was their most successful ship. She obtained an annual average catch of 125 tuns of oil and five tons of whalebone, considerably better than the national average which was 84 tuns of oil and 4.2 tons of whalebone between 1800 and 1804.[13]

Middleton appears to have earned an average of almost £5,000 per season between 1801-1811, or about £15 per ton. Despite this, *Middleton*'s earnings were significantly less than those of *Henrietta* which averaged almost £25 per ton during the same period.[14] The disparity in earnings between the two vessels raises a number of interesting questions about optimum vessel size. Despite obtaining greater annual average catches than the smaller vessels whaling from Whitby for most of the period (see Table 15), large Tyne whalers like *Middleton* (320 tons) and *Isabella* (346 tons) still struggled to maintain their profitability. Higher maintenance costs, particularly in respect of the wages and provisions of a larger crew, additional equipment and insurance premiums clearly reduced the competitive advantage of large vessels. At 250 tons, for example, the Bounty Acts obliged the owners of *Henrietta* to carry five whaleboats, whereas *Middleton* and *Isabella* both carried six. The better earning and seasonal performance of *Henrietta* demonstrates that additional whaleboats did not give larger vessels an advantage. Since the whaling vessels at Newcastle in 1805 were significantly larger than those at Whitby averaging 330 tons compared to 272 tons,[15] the lower cost advantages of the Whitby ships together with their better earnings may go some way to explaining the greater success and consistency of interest at that port. When the number of ships sailing to the Greenland Fishery from Newcastle declined from nine in 1807, to three in 1811, the number of whalers at Whitby remained at seven (see Table 15).

Katherine was sold to London in 1808 where she continued to be employed as a whaler. *Isabella* was lost in the Gulf of St. Lawrence in 1810 and *Middleton* sold to the Aberdeen Whale Fishery Company the following year.[16] The Humbles sold all of their interests in the whale oil yard and warehouse facilities at Felling Shore at the same time. The commercial experience of John and James Humble as well as that of Thomas and Edward Hurry, suggests that the operation of several ships as part of a small whaling fleet did not always bring financial rewards.

The most successful vessels in the Tyne fleet between 1804 and 1811 were *Lady Jane* and *Euretta*, both financed by general shipowners. *Euretta* was built at Newcastle in 1775 and introduced to the Greenland trade in 1798 after a short period in the Transport Service. Her captain, John Boswell (1769-1819) was an experienced

Table 15. A comparison of whaling performance of Newcastle and Whitby vessels, 1800-1811

	Whitby	*Newcastle*	*Whitby*		*Newcastle*	
			Average per ship			
Year	*Number of vessels*		*Oil (tuns)*	*Bone (tons)*	*Oil (tuns)*	*Bone (tons)*
1800	4	3	89	4	122	8
1801	4	5	85	3	132	9
1802	6	7	93	3	223	11
1803	7	11	76	3	100	6
1804	7	10	85	2	163	9
1805	9	9	130	4	143	7
1806	7	9	101	3	128	5
1807	7	9	116	4	140	4
1808	7	6	161	4	155	4
1809	6	5	127	4	138	4
1810	7	5	135	5	188	7
1811	7	3	168	5	120	5

Source: PRO, ZHC 1/772. Accounts relating to the Whale Fisheries, BPP, 1823.

whalerman from North Shields who purchased the ship outright in 1804.[17] Boswell was the only owner-operator to sail in the Tyne whaling fleet during the French Wars and clearly had a vested interest in the success of his ship. In 1801, *Euretta* secured fifteen whales producing 414 casks of blubber, and twelve tons of whalebone. The cargo represented a monetary value of £6,480,[18] and compared favourably with the successful Scottish whalers of 1801, *Raith* and *Eliza Swan.*[19] At Whitby Scoresby computed the earnings of *Resolution* to have been £6,810 per season over fourteen seasons between 1804 and 1818.[20] *Euretta* averaged £6,376 per season. It was more than enough to cover expenses and realise seasonal profits. In 1811, Boswell sold *Euretta* to London merchants, but purchased an interest in two other whalers; *Eliza*, 311 tons, which he commanded personally until 1818, and *British Queen*, 362 tons. Both vessels sailed annually from the Tyne between 1812 and 1822.

Lady Jane, 313 tons, was undoubtedly the most successful whaler at Newcastle during these years. Already an old ship when she was introduced to the trade on Tyneside in 1804, *Lady Jane* was built on the river Thames in 1772. Jointly owned by William Linskill of Tynemouth and Quentin Blackburn of Newcastle, *Lady Jane*, commanded by William Holmes, an experienced Greenland veteran, sailed consistently to the Davis Straits and returned the highest average catch of any vessel in the Tyne fleet; 178 tuns of oil and more than eight tons of whalebone. Earnings exceeded those of *Euretta* for much of the period, suggesting perhaps, like the vessels at Berwick, that Davis Straits ships had a higher earnings potential than those that sailed for Greenland. *Lady Jane* was particularly successful after 1810, when cargoes valued at more than £9,000 were regularly secured. In 1813, *Lady Jane* was the most successful ship in the national whaling fleet in terms of the monetary value of her catch. In that year, the oil and bone value of her cargo of thirteen large Davis Straits whales realised £13,000 for her owners '*...the greatest profit ever made by one vessel in any one season since the Northern Whale Fishery was practised.*'[21]

It was also a memorable year in the history of Whitby whaling. On 2 February 1813, *Esk* was launched from the yard of Fishburn and Broderick. Purpose-built for William Scoresby Jnr. at a cost of £14,000 she was a ship-rigged vessel of 354 tons. *Esk* carried seven whaleboats and mustered her crew of 40 men on 12 March. She was ready for sea by 16 March but had considerable difficulty in reaching it.

> '*Tuesday, 16 March 1813*
> *At 3 p.m. the tide was high water, we have a considerable strain on the hawser, but could not get the ship over the bank. The* Aimwell, William and Ann, Lively *and* Henrietta *being of lighter draught and in a more convenient situation got to sea. During the next ebb we got 6 or 8 of our men to dig away the outside raised part of the ground which prevented the ship moving out of the dock she had formed with her weight. At 4 p.m. [the following day] by mere strength of power we drew the ship forward into the deepest water of the channel...about this time the remaining two fishing ships the* Resolution *and the* Volunteer *sailed to sea and we were left alone.*'[22]

Esk grounded once more before she reached Whitby bridge and her owners became anxious of the possibility of the ship being neaped in the harbour. Drastic measures were called for. Rather than lighten the ship of her stores and equipment, Scoresby lashed two lighters to *Esk*, one on each side. Their buoyancy lifted the ship sufficiently for it to be hauled passed Whitby bridge into the outer harbour at high water on 18 March.

'Thursday, 18 March 1813
...by the assistance of a rope to the pier, two foy boats and a light breeze of wind we were drawn safely without the piers at 5 p.m.'

It had taken two full days of constant effort to get *Esk* to sea. On the following day Scoresby recorded triumphantly:

'Friday, 19 March 1813
...Delightful clear weather, steering N.E by E under all the sails that we could display.'

Esk reached Shetland on 21 March where she remained a fortnight before sailing on a successful maiden voyage to the Greenland whaling grounds. It turned out to be a successful year for the Whitby fleet and there was general rejoicing in the town when the ships returned:

'Arrived at Whitby on the 13 inst. from Greenland the Esk, *Scoresby, 15 fish, 508 butts;* Aimwell, *Johnson, 7 fish, 180 butts;* Henrietta, *Kearsley, 11 fish, 280 butts;* Volunteer, *Dawson, 7 fish, 192 butts...'* [23]

The remaining vessels arrived at the port during the rest of August with the produce of 24 whales. The official totals imported at Whitby in 1813 amounted to 826 tuns of whale oil and 33.5 tons of whalebone worth £32,562 at average prices.[24]

The end of the Napoleonic War in 1815 was not followed by the rapid expansion of the national whaling fleet that had characterised the end of the American War in 1783. The number of vessels sailing to the Arctic grounds certainly rose, by 45 per cent overall, between 1810 and 1815, but the increase did not correspond to the end of the war. It was principally accounted for by the expansion of the Hull fleet and the development of interest at a number of Scottish ports. At Whitby, however, the whaling fleet continued to expand in the post-war years. By 1819, there were thirteen ships sailing from the river Esk making Whitby the third-ranking English whaling port after Hull and London. Unlike Whitby, Newcastle's relative importance as a whaling port declined. In 1816, Tyne-based ships represented just 4 per cent of the national whaling fleet, lower than at any time since 1774. Newcastle shipowners fitted-out five to six ships per annum between 1814-1821. Amongst these were a number of 'new' ships and masters including, *Cove*, Captain George Palmer, and *Grenville Bay* which sailed from the Tyne on her maiden whaling voyage in 1816. Built at Stockton in 1783, *Grenville Bay* had been employed as a West Indies trader throughout the French Wars. Two Sunderland owned ships, *Cerberus* and *Leviathan*, also sailed as part of the Tyne fleet between 1814-1817. Both vessels were owned by John and Philip Laing, members of one of the best known shipbuilding families of the river Wear. *Leviathan* was foreign built and taken as a prize during the American War of 1812. *Cerberus* was newly built and appears to have undertaken her maiden voyage to the Arctic whaling grounds in 1816.[25] However, despite the success of the Fishery in general, they appear to have been unprofitable ships. In four voyages between 1814 and 1817 *Leviathan* and *Cerberus* secured 200 tuns of whale oil and a total income of £2,000 per voyage, hardly sufficient to cover their expenses. *Leviathan* suffered considerable wear and tear. Scoresby on *Esk* recorded damage to the Tyneside ship in 1814:

> *'27 April 1814. Lat.78°29' Long.6°10'E*
> *The* Leviathan *of Shields in working to windward in the morning run against a piece of ice which has stove her very severely, breaking 14 timbers and leaving an indented wound 14 feet long.'* [26]

Leviathan was subsequently wrecked in the ice with three other ships in May 1817. John and Philip Laing did not replace her, choosing instead to abandon their brief and unprofitable association with the Greenland trade. Sunderland's direct connection with Arctic enterprise came to an end with the loss of *Leviathan*. In terms of their annual performance, however, the whalers of Newcastle and Whitby continued to exceed the national average of catches[27] in the years which followed the end of the Napoleonic War. It undoubtedly reflected the degree of skill and experience then existing amongst the captains and crews of local whalers.

Berwick-upon-Tweed 1807-1825

The development of a small whaling industry at Berwick after 1807 coincided with an expansion of the port and its facilities at the beginning of the nineteenth century.[28] Berwick had great commercial importance for the Borders region and became the focus of an extensive trade in salmon, grain and other agricultural produce. As a subsidiary whaling port, Berwick complemented the whaling fleets of Newcastle and Whitby. Its fishing tradition and a steady demand for whale products, especially whale oil, in the Scottish Borders helped to sustain whaling from the port.

The arrival of two whalers at Berwick in 1807 coincided with the reduction of fleet numbers elsewhere. The withdrawal of whaling ships from Dunbar may also have been significant since it left Berwick as the only whaling port between Newcastle and Leith. *Norfolk*, 309 tons, had been one of the whalers owned by Edward and Thomas Hurry at Howdonpans and was transferred to Berwick after the failure of

Table 16. Catches and estimated earnings of the Berwick whalers, 1813-1822

	No. of ships						
Year	*Green-land*	*Davis Straits*	*Oil (tuns)*	*Bone (tons)*	*Total value (£)*	*Value per ship (£)*	*Earnings per ton (£)*
1813	1	1	251	11.4	9,902	4,951	19
1814	1	1	177	9.8	7,097	3,548	14
1815	1	1	78	3.7	3,087	1,543	7
1816	2	-	150	5.8	5,852	2,926	12
1817	2	-	76	3.5	3,001	1,500	6
1818	1	1	133	6.25	3,027	1,513	7
1819	1	1	210	10.3	4,814	2,407	10
1820	1	1	308	16.1	7,140	3,570	14
1821	1	1	221	10.2	5,015	2,507	10
1822	2	-	41	1.5	1,056	528	3

Source: PRO, ZHC 1/772. Accounts relating to the Whale Fisheries, BPP, 1823.

Notes

Average price of whale-oil	£36.5/tun	1813-17
	£19/tun	1818-21
Average price of whalebone	£65/ton	1814-17
	£80/ton	1818-21
	£185/ton	1822

Earnings per ton includes the bounty at twenty shillings per ton.

their shipbuilding business. The other ship, *Lively*, 238 tons, was already owned and registered at Berwick prior to her introduction to the Greenland trade. Both ships were financed by the same group of owners. Two of them, John Miller Dickson and James Hogarth, had substantial business and shipowning interests at the port including their investment in the Old Shipping Company which operated Berwick smacks. Another, Thomas Richard Batson, was a banker who subsequently developed an interest in whaling at Newcastle. *Norfolk* and *Lively* were the largest vessels on the Berwick register in 1811. They used the Carr Rock anchorage at Spittal to discharge their cargoes and the whale oil was processed at a Greenland yard located at the head of Spittal Sands. Uniquely, the Berwick whalers used the first of the ebb tide to discharge their cargoes. Barrels of blubber were pitched over the side of the ships into the Tweed and carried by the tide to Spittal Strand where they were collected for processing.

The experience of shipowners at Newcastle and Whitby suggested that the smaller of the two whalers at Berwick, *Lively*, would become a more profitable ship than

Norfolk. Lower outfitting costs and a shorter whaling season facilitated the employment of the Greenland ship in late season voyages to the Baltic or in the coal trade. In 1823, for example, *Lively* returned from Greenland on 8 September with the produce of four whales, sailed to Riga with a cargo of herrings on 27 September and delivered timber from there at London in December. *Lively* was back at Berwick in early January.[29] Late season voyages such as these were crucial to the profitability of the ship since *Lively* was not a successful whaler and failed to match the earnings of similar Greenland ships at Whitby and Hull. The average annual income of the Berwick whalers between 1815 and 1819 was about £1,977, substantially less than the Hull ships and sufficient only to realise moderate profits during occasional years.[30] In the light of this indifferent success, the persistence of whaling from Berwick during these years is difficult to explain. It probably reflected an absence of alternative sources of employment for the ships during a period of depression and over-capacity in the shipping industry. Either way, it was clearly unfortunate that when the Berwick owners finally decided to send *Lively* to the Davis Straits in 1825, the vessel was immediately wrecked in the ice. A demonstration, perhaps, that chance continued to play its part in the success or failure of commercial decisions.

References

1. Jackson, G. *The British Whaling Trade*, Appendix 4.

2. Young, Revd. G. *A History of Whitby*, (1817), p.567.

3. Young, G. *History of Whitby*, p.566.

4. Jones, S. 'A Maritime History of the Port of Whitby', University of London, Ph.D (1982), p.285.

5. Jones, S. 'Port of Whitby', Ph.D, p.286. In addition to a successful career at Whitby, William Scoresby Snr. commanded whaleships at London, Greenock and Hull before he retired from the sea in 1823.

6. Account Books of the ship *Henrietta* of Whitby (1776-1820), National Maritime Museum (NMM), AMS/35.

7. Jones, S. 'Port of Whitby', Ph.D, p.286.

8. Jackson, G. *Hull in the Eighteenth Century*, p.162.

9. *Norfolk* was transferred to Berwick owners in 1807 and began a distinguished whaling career from that port which lasted until 1837.

10. McCord, N. *North East England:The Region's Growth and Development*, (Batsford, 1979), p.48.

11. Losses are calculated on the basis of fitting-out expenses of £13 per ton and are derived from the Account Books of the ship *Henrietta* of Whitby, NMM, AMS/35.

12. *Katherine* was a former Dutch whaler, *Hollandia*, which was captured off Shetland by a British warship and subsequently sold as a prize in 1803.

13. Jackson, G. *Whaling Trade*, Table 3, p.82.

14. Account Books of the ship *Henrietta* of Whitby, NMM, AMS/35.

15. Accounts relating to the Whale Fisheries, Public Record Office (PRO), ZHC 1/772, BPP, (1823).

16. *Middleton* continued her career as a whaler at Aberdeen and was eventually wrecked in Baffin Bay during the notorious whaling season of 1830.

17. Tyne Wear Archives Dept. (TWAD), EX/NC/1/2, No. 21, 1804.

18. *Newcastle Chronicle*, 11 July 1801. Using the bone yield of *Euretta*'s cargo as an indicator of the size of her catch, this could well be an underestimate of the actual earnings of the ship

19. Jackson, G. *Whaling Trade*, p.85.

20. Scoresby, W. *Arctic Regions*, II, p.395.

21. Scoresby, *Arctic Regions*, II, p.123.

22. Journal of a Greenland voyage in the new ship *Esk* of and from Whitby in the year 1813, William Scoresby commander, Whitby Literary and Philosophical Society (WLPS).

23. *Newcastle Courant*, 21 August 1813.

24. Accounts relating to the Whale Fisheries, PRO, ZHC 1/772, BPP, 1823 and Jackson, G. *Whaling Trade*, p.118.

25. TWAD, Ex/Sul/3, No. 26, 1814 and No. 17, 1816. *Cerberus* undertook a single voyage to the Greenland Fishery in 1816. Thereafter she was employed as an East Indiaman and was wrecked in Table Bay, Cape of Good Hope in 1821.

26. William Scoresby, 'Journal of a voyage to Greenland in the ship *Esk* of Whitby, 1814' Stamp, T & C. *Greenland Voyager*. p.152

27. Scoresby estimated these to be 91.4 tuns of oil for English ships and 96.3 tuns for Scottish ships. The averages at Whitby and Newcastle between 1814-1817 were 111 and 103.7 respectively. Scoresby, W. *Arctic Regions*, II, p.131 and Accounts Relating to the Whale Fisheries, BPP, 1823.

28. The Berwick Harbour Act was passed in 1808 and the pier built in 1810.

29. *Newcastle Chronicle*, 20 September; 4 October; 8 November 1823 and 3 January 1824.

30. Jackson calculated the five-year average value of the catch of Hull whalers to be £3,488 between 1815-1819. See Jackson, G. *Whaling Trade*, Table 11, p.126.

5

'...Is not the light from the oil lamps sufficiently vivid for every purpose of the tradesman?'

[Handbill addressed to the citizens of North Shields, 1820]

Greenland Yards and Greenland Products

By the beginning of the nineteenth century Greenland whaling was predominantly an east coast activity and the continued participation of local vessels had considerable economic and social importance for the region. The commercial and industrial activity generated by the Greenland trade represented much more than the employment of ships and seaman. It sustained a processing and distribution industry of considerable value and provided employment for hundreds of shore-based workers. In addition, Greenland ships generally made heavy demands on port industries like ship repairing and outfitting and they required a constant supply of the products of ancillary industries like boat building, rope making and marine metalworking. The harpoons and lances manufactured by Pow and Fawcus of North Shields were commonly used by most British whalers, just as Whitby-built ships might be found whaling from almost any port. The products of the Greenland trade also found extensive national and international markets.

Whale oil had a variety of industrial, institutional and domestic uses and had been used in the region for generations.[1] Indeed, growth in the consumption of whale oil during the second half of the eighteenth century was one of a number of indicators of the accelerating industrial activity and population growth of that period. As demand for raw materials increased the whaling industry benefited directly, as one writer put it: *'Every new piece of machinery needed lubricants, every new household needed light...'*.[2]

Whale oil was one of the principal sources of lighting in the mines, workshops and factories of the Industrial Revolution. It was widely used as an illuminant in shops, churches and institutional buildings, and was increasingly utilised in street lighting, particularly towards the end of the eighteenth century. Whale oil was also used in the manufacture of cheap woollen cloth, in sailmaking, tanning and metalworking. It was a basic ingredient of paints and varnishes, and used extensively in the manufacture of soap. The expanding and industrialising economy of north-east England contained most of these activities, and they provided a significant demand for the products of the Whale Fishery. Its use as an illuminant probably reached a peak about 1820 and consumption may have accounted for as much as 40 per cent of the annual product of local ships. Thereafter, the increasing use of coal gas reduced this area of demand. In soap making, the Tyneside demand for whale oil peaked between 1825 and 1840 when it may have taken up to 15 per cent of the annual product. Leather making and tanning were also small but significant local industries and they provided a consistent demand for whale oil, amounting to perhaps 10 per cent of the total obtained.[3] The accumulated consumption of shipbuilding, rope making, textiles, paint and varnish manufacture probably accounted for much of the remainder of the whale oil used within the region. As a commodity, whale oil also entered the trade of ports like Whitby and Newcastle.

The annual productivity of ships engaged in the Greenland trade was notoriously unpredictable and the amounts of blubber obtained for processing varied from year to year. In 1762 Newcastle ships obtained just ten tuns of whale oil and in 1792 the whalers at Sunderland returned 'clean'. By contrast, Tyne whalers procured 1,600 tuns of whale oil in 1804 and imports at Whitby exceeded 1,000 tuns for the first time in 1805. During the Napoleonic War, and just after, individual Greenland ships regularly secured large and valuable cargoes. In 1813, for example, *Lady Jane* returned to the Tyne from the Davis Straits with a cargo estimated to be worth £13,000. In 1815 the same ship:

> *'...brought to Shields a whale which...filled casks which held 10,050 gallons. It is supposed the largest whale ever brought into this port and at a moderate calculation is now worth £1,500.'*[4]

Unlike their American and South Sea cousins, Arctic whalers returned with the blubber of the whales they had killed. Their cargoes were then discharged and processed before any whale oil could be marketed. Accordingly, all of the whaling ports in the region had at least one oil yard with sufficient capacity to deal with the trade of the port. There was an oil yard at Stockton-on-Tees between 1786 and 1793 and at Berwick-upon-Tweed between 1807 and 1837 even though both ports committed no more than two vessels to the trade. There were two 'Greenland' yards at Sunderland between 1785 and 1798, at Monkwearmouth and Hylton Ferry; on the Tyne there were yards at Saltmeadows, Felling Shore, Howdonpans and North Shields. The 'blubber houses' at Whitby were situated on the west side of the Esk on the same site that was later occupied by the gas works. These oil yards were relatively simple affairs and, in the early years at least, did not involve a substantial investment. When the owners of *Disko Bay* entered the Davis Straits trade in 1784, they built a small oil-house on Felling Shore from the profits of the first voyage. Initial construction costs amounted to £667 and further sums were subsequently expended in the construction of a warehouse and ancillary buildings in 1786-87.[5] According to Scoresby, writing in 1820, whale oil processing premises normally consisted of a single copper vessel of between three and ten tuns capacity, fixed six to ten feet above the ground, together with an adjoining back or cooler, built generally of wood, occasionally of brick or stone, lined with lead or cement, and capable of containing between ten and twenty tuns of whale oil. Up to five additional storage chambers, depending upon the trade of the port, was sometimes provided. Greenland yards usually had their own quay with cranes and ancillary equipment, together with warehouses, cooperage and dwelling house. Scoresby continued:

> '...*in most of the outports the oil is generally deposited in casks, in which it remains until it is disposed of by the importers. In London, however, and in some concerns at Hull and other ports, the speculators in the whale fishery are provided with cisterns or tanks wherein they can deposit their oil and preserve it until a convenient time for selling.*' [6]

The first whale oil manufactory to be established in the North-East was at Saltmeadows near Gateshead on the south bank of the Tyne. It was constructed for the Newcastle Whale Fishing Company on land leased from the Corporation and opened in June 1752. Saltmeadows remained one of the principal sites of whale oil manufacture on the Tyne until 1831. The first whale oil yard at Whitby was established in 1753.

The processing of blubber into whale oil was not a time consuming affair. Each copper was charged with blubber and then brought to the boil. The contents, which were occasionally stirred by boilermen with long wooden poles, would not usually be boiled for more than three or four hours. Each copper was boiled twice in 24 hours and a cargo of up to 150 tuns could be processed in three to four days. In 1807 the blubber cargoes of the Berwick whalers, *Lively* and *Norfolk*, were processed into whale oil and advertised for sale within a month of their arrival at the port.[7] The smell emitted from the process was said to turn strong men pale and make brave men weep! In hot and humid conditions with a breeze from an unfavourable direction the atmosphere of whaling ports at the end of the season was usually thick with the foetid stench of processing blubber.

Whale oil was usually marketed by merchants directly associated with the whaling ships, or by oil merchants whose names frequently appeared in local trade directories. Advertisements announcing the sale or availability of whale oil generally appeared in the late summer and autumn editions of local newspapers. Since the marketing of whale oil depended upon the seasonal success of local whalers it was subject to regular price fluctuations. During the eighteenth century when whale oil was stored and sold in casks, merchants and manufacturers often bought in advance of their immediate needs. The development of more sophisticated storage facilities enabled independent merchants to adopt a more flexible approach and they could release whale oil onto the market at almost any time of the year.

The arrangement of equipment required to render blubber into whale oil conformed to the 'tower' system in which the raw materials to be manufactured were lifted to the top of the plant and processed at correspondingly lower levels until the finished product was put into storage. The brewing industry used a similar system and coppers of about the same capacity as those used in whale oil manufacture. Indeed, there appears to have been few technical difficulties in converting equipment from oil processing to brewing and back again. Dual purpose breweries and whale oil manufacturies maximised the use of equipment which was common to both. Brewers rarely attempted to brew ale between July and September because of the difficulties associated with controlling the fermentation process. By contrast, whale oil processing was an activity confined to the summer months. Moreover, many brewers invested in shipping because of the advantages it gave them in the transportation of raw materials and the distribution of finished products. On Tyneside there were numerous examples of brewers who invested in whaling ships—Samuel Hurry at Howdonpans, John Humble at Felling Shore and George Barras at South Shields, a founder of the Newcastle Brewery.

After brewing, whale oil manufacture had its closest connection with soap making. Whale oil was a basic ingredient of industrial soft soaps and soap makers, like brewers, used similar equipment to that used in the Greenland yards. The first large soap manufactory on Tyneside was established by Thomas Doubleday and Anthony Easterby about 1790. Both men were important industrial innovators and pioneers of modern alkali manufacture on Tyneside.[8] Their original premises were located at The Close in Newcastle adjacent to the Mansion House. However, the disagreeable smells emitted from the soapery '*...resembling the smell of rotten eggs, gas and onions...*'[9] was the cause of constant litigation with the Corporation. Doubleday and Easterby, who had a direct interest in the whale oil procured by local ships, were eventually persuaded to lease the oil yard at Saltmeadows in 1812. They converted it to the manufacture of sulphuric acid in 1831.[10]

Despite the importance of the soap-making industry as a consumer of whale oil, the greatest demand undoubtedly came from the ubiquitous oil lamps of the Industrial Revolution. Considerable quantities of whale oil were used as an illuminant by public and private consumers. Collieries were particularly heavy users. The proprietors of Walker Colliery, for example, regularly purchased between ten to thirteen tuns annually from the owners of *Disko Bay* during the late 1780s.[11] Walker Colliery, sunk in 1765, was the first of a new generation of deep pits fringing the banks of the Tyne below Newcastle. There were others at Willington (1775), Felling (1779), Wallsend Main (1781), Hebburn (1794), Percy Main (1802), Jarrow (1803) and South Shields (1810). All of these pits were deeper than 100 fathoms.[12] Cumulative annual consumption of whale oil at these pits alone probably represented 10 per cent of the amount carried into the Tyne by local whalers during the opening decade of the nineteenth century.

The principal urban centres and market towns of the region had whale oil street lamps. There were over 200 in Newcastle by 1817, lit between September and March. They consumed up to 600 gallons of oil per season. The Durham Paving Commissioners maintained about the same number of whale oil street lamps in the city between 1790 and 1824. They usually obtained their supply from Tyneside, but occasionally from Hull as well. In 1816, 1817 and 1819, John Milburn & Co. of North Shields, principal owners of the whalers *British Queen* and *Grenville Bay* were the suppliers.[13] In 1818, Messrs. Batson supplied 551 gallons of whale oil.[14] Estimates for the supply of 600 gallons of oil were sought from eight to ten merchants in June 1820. The contract was awarded to Ralph Wilkinson of Hull.[15] The lowest price of best Greenland whale oil was sought from Wilkinson in 1821, but the order went to William Anderson of Newcastle at £23 per tun.[16] Wilkinson was more successful in 1822 with a price of £23 per tun delivered free at Newcastle.[17]

Since a tun of whale oil consisted of 252 gallons,[18] the lamps at Newcastle and Durham collectively consumed less than six tuns per annum, hardly a significant amount at a time when individual ships were returning with cargoes of between 150-200 tuns. At Morpeth, where oil lamps were first installed in 1793, only 63 gallons of oil at £22 per tun was needed during the first season.[19] A similar amount was consumed the following year. Nevertheless, the cumulative demand of small market towns like Pickering, Guisborough, Morpeth and Hexham, together with institutional, industrial and domestic demands, accounted for the bulk of the whale oil used for lighting. In addition the increasing use of whale oil for navigational lights and lighthouses became a feature of the late eighteenth and early nineteenth centuries. The Mersey lights established in 1763, burnt whale oil in flat-wicked burners. By 1800 there were 28 lighthouses around the coasts of the United

Kingdom that burnt whale oil in a similar manner. The High and Low Lights at North Shields, constructed in 1808, burnt whale oil using the Argand principle invented in 1784. The Argand burner had a tubular wick which drew a current of air through the centre, thereby aerating the flame and producing a ten-fold increase in the brilliance of light provided by a single wick. It was an invention of special importance to lighthouses.

The consumption of whale oil for street lighting reached a peak about 1820. Thereafter the increasing use of coal gas as a lighting agent broke the monopoly that the oil merchants once enjoyed. At Newcastle, Anthony Clapham proposed to light the town with gas in May 1817 and the transition from whale oil to coal gas had been made by 1822. North Shields was lit by gas in October 1820 and Berwick in January 1822. By 1826 most towns in the North-East that had formerly utilised whale oil lamps for street lighting, had made the transition to coal gas. Oil merchants were naturally opposed to this development and they fought a rearguard action. In 1820, a handbill addressed to the inhabitants of North Shields asked them to consider the advantages they derived from the port's association with the whaling trade, and concluded:

> *'…it appears to be a difficult task to adduce any argument or reason why the public of North Shields should give their countenance and support to the introduction of a novelty, which, while it can yield them no advantage, has a direct tendency to stop the source from whence a great proportion of their prosperity flows…is not the light from the oil lamps sufficiently vivid for every purpose of the tradesman?'*[20]

The supply of whale oil to small businesses, churches and industrial concerns accounted for the bulk of oil that went to lighting and the loss of this business caused most anxiety to merchants:

> *'Gas Company profits were heavily dependent upon the consumption of business concerns since street lighting contracts were generally considered to give little remuneration.'*[21]

Once the gas companies had broken through to the private consumer, the oil merchants lost one of their principal markets. Nevertheless, whale oil continued to be used in many rural areas for a number of years to come. Moreover, the continued use of whale oil in soap, paint and leather manufacture secured its survival as an industrial raw material well into the nineteenth century.

At Whitby and Hull oil merchants fought back by developing a system of manufacturing gas from whale oil. The streets of Whitby were first lit by oil gas in

November 1825 when Gideon Buck established a gas company on Church Street at the bottom of the Horse Road. Buck's experiment was short lived however, and replaced by orthodox coal gas about 1837. In rural areas inferior whale oil and blubber had agricultural uses, as ingredients in composts and fertilisers:

> '*...the application of...whale blubber, the bottoms and refuse of oil casks etc. when blended with earthy materials, so as to be laid upon the land in an even and regular manner...have been found, by the experiments of different cultivators to form very strong and powerful manures.*'[22]

Experiments with oil composts were undertaken as early as 1769 and they were widely used in some districts by the beginning of the nineteenth century.[23] One recipe incorporated fourteen gallons of whale oil into compost suitable for an acre of land. Opinions of its usefulness varied and the expense involved, even using waste oil and blubber was a considerable disadvantage to its widespread adoption.

The manufacture and supply of whale oil was the principal concern of most whaler owners, but they also gained considerable commercial advantages from the preparation and sale of whalebone which was worth £350 per ton in 1770. Whalebone was esteemed for its combination of strength, elasticity and lightness. It could be cut and moulded into almost any shape and had a variety of uses. It was sometimes used by cabinet makers, watchmakers and precision instrument manufacturers, as well as by saddlers, haberdashers, carriage and harness makers. In later years whalebones were widely used as monumental gate posts, once a common sight in the hinterland of whaling ports. An advertisement of 1773 was fairly typical:

> '*Whalebone*
> *Manufactured in all its branches at the Folly, Newcastle, by William Coulson and Company, haberdashers, staymakers and whipmakers and all dealers in that article will have every advantage in price and quality.*' [24]

Whalebone became more valuable as it increased in length and width. According to Scoresby, the 'size' bone of six feet or upwards in length was sold for the highest prices, and the remaining 'under-size' packed into portable bundles consisting of about one hundredweight each, and sold for half the price. Because of its great value, whalebone was carefully cleaned and prepared before marketing and usually removed to a central warehouse where it was carefully stored. A building in St. Nicholas' churchyard in Newcastle was utilised as a whalebone warehouse after 1759.[25] The proprietors, Messrs. Jorden, Scott and Company maintained contacts with the Hull and London markets where much of Newcastle's whalebone was shipped.

The whaling ports of north-east England, particularly Whitby, traded extensively in whale products. In 1790 over half of the whalebone and almost two-thirds of the whale oil obtained by the Whitby ships in that year was traded coastwise from the port.[26] The bulk of it went to London, but in subsequent years when fewer ports equipped their own whaling fleets, Whitby came to supply a much broader market.[27] The same was true of Berwick-upon-Tweed whose merchants accessed an extensive market in the Scottish Borders. Tyne trade delivered whale products to destinations at home and abroad although, as a proportion of the annual product, the amount traded coastwise from the Tyne was substantially less than it was at Whitby. It did not exceed 130 tuns in a single year (1788-89) and averaged about 10 per cent per annum for selected years between 1754-55 and 1789-90.[28] There was also a foreign trade in whale products from the river Tyne. The *Disko Bay* accounts certainly indicate regular shipments of oil and whalebone to destinations in northern Europe between 1786 and 1793,[29] and the trade clearly persisted well into the 1820s.

This direct trade in whale products was only part of the picture. The Greenland trade also generated substantial amounts of business through the outfitting, victualling and general maintenance costs of the whaling ships themselves. The business was just as lucrative to farmers and grocers as it was to tradesmen and merchants. Whitby whalers benefited farming districts in the North Yorkshire Moors and the Vale of Pickering which supplied beef, pork, eggs, cheese and cereal. The owners of *Henrietta*, for example, appear to have purchased '*piggs at Pickering*' annually, throughout the period covered by their accounts (1776-1820). The pigs were slaughtered at Pickering, salted down, and transported to Whitby by 'old Tom Dobson', the local carrier and waggonman who appears to have delivered farm produce to the ship for almost 40 years. Costs and expenses for salt pork alone amounted to over £200 in 1802 and *Henrietta* was not a large whaler.[30] In January and February 1780, Kenneth Thompson, master of *John and Margaret*, purchased two tons of hard bread and five hundredweight of barley from Peter Dale, a ships' stores merchant at North Shields.[31] Similarly, in 1786 the owners of *Disko Bay* purchased supplies from butchers, grocers, bakers, tallow chandlers, druggists and brewers. The cost of the beer and ale amounted to £60 and the debit side of the account book in 1786 recorded transactions of over £2,200.

Greenland seamen clearly had prodigious appetites and whaler captains were frequently obliged to purchase additional stores from other ships:

> *'9 June 1818, Lat. 76°10'N*
> *Finding our provisions rapidly on the decrease we took an estimate of what was expended and what was left...we found that in 70 days, 50 men had consumed 6,820lbs. of beef and pork,*

4,700lbs. of bread, 1,200lbs. of flour, 400lbs. of oatmeal, a large quantity of pease and barley and about 50 bushels of potatoes ...and on some occasions the crew complained of not having sufficient...'[32]

Tradesmen of various descriptions always figured prominently in the maintenance of whalers—plumbers, coopers, blacksmiths, blockmakers, sailmakers and carpenters. Marine metalworking was especially important to the whaling fleet and a number of local companies, as well as individuals, acquired a national reputation as harpoon makers—Hawks, Crawshay and Co. of Gateshead, Ambrose Crowley & Co. of Winlaton, Pow and Fawcus of North Shields. The latter, which was certainly the best known, was founded by Robert Flinn at Hartley in Northumberland at the end of the eighteenth century. Flinn was a contemporary of another famous harpoon maker, William Carr (1756-1825), the so-called Blyth Sampson. Carr was reputed to have made his harpoons from iron recovered from old horse shoe nails gathered from various smithies in the neighbourhood of Blyth and Seaton Sluice. Carr's harpoons were so malleable that they stretched and twisted, rather than snapped under the tremendous loads exerted upon them during the capture of a whale. The region also boasted one of the best known innovators in the development of gun harpoons, William Greener. He was a gunsmith who began his experiments on Tyneside. Most of the vessels in the British whaling fleet carried at least one of Greener's gun harpoons by the 1830s as well as the additional paraphernalia common to Arctic whalers of that period. When the 'fishing stores' of *Norfolk* were sold at Berwick in October 1838 they included:

'360 casks, 6 whaleboats, 53 harpoons, 5 split-gun harpoons, 1 harpoon gun, 7 beard harpoons, 46 harpoon stocks, 22 blubber knives, 17 blubber spades, 49 lances as well as boats axes, ice-saws, blubber hooks and surgeon's implements...'[33]

One contemporary source estimated that five whalers sailing from the river Tyne in 1820 expended about £3,000 per ship in wages and provisions, most of which was spent in the locality. In addition to the seamen who manned these whaleships at least 500 'Greenlanders' were employed in the ships of other ports, who, it was estimated, earned £12,000 which was subsequently spent in the Tyneside communities.[34] Collectively, the five whalers sailing from the river Tyne in 1820 probably generated £15-£20,000 of business, over and above the value of the whale products they were able to procure. In the same year Whitby sustained a fleet of eleven ships and Berwick had two. Clearly, the participation of local vessels in the Arctic Whale Fishery had enormous significance for the local economy of these ports as well.

References

1. At the end of the fifteenth century the Company of Merchant Adventurers of Newcastle included wholesale merchants who traded in '… *train oil and other Baltic products…*'.

2. Lythe, S.G.E. 'The Dundee Whale Fishery', *Scottish Journal of Political Economy*, II, (1964), pp.158-169.

3. Barrow, A. 'North East Coast Whale Fishery, 1750-1850', University of Northumbria, Ph.D. (1989), Part I, Chap.IV.

4. *Newcastle Courant*, 9 September 1815.

5. Barrow, T. 'The Account Books of the ship *Disko Bay* of Newcastle 1784-1802: A case study of vessel management, costs and profitability in the British shipping industry', *The Mariners Mirror*, Vol. 81 (1995), pp.171-181.

6. Scoresby, W. *Arctic Regions*, II, p.407.

7. In 1807, *Lively* docked at Berwick with the blubber of seventeen whales on 6 August, and the whale oil derived from the cargo, 130 tuns, was advertised for sale on 3 September. *Norfolk* returned on 11 August and her whale oil cargo, 98 tuns, advertised on 12 September.

8. Doubleday and Easterby experimented with lead-lined chambers in the manufacture of sulphuric acid, an essential ingredient in the production of alkali. Their association with the Greenland yard at Saltmeadows, which certainly had lead-lined chambers, suggests a correlation between these processes hitherto unappreciated by historians of the chemical industry.

9. Tyne Wear Archives Dept.(TWAD), Minutes of Newcastle Common Council–indictment for nuisance–August 1829.

10. TWAD, Minutes of Newcastle Common Council, March 1828 and September 1831.

11. Northumberland Record Office (NRO), Blackett (Wylam). Account book of the ship *Disko Bay*. Entries for 18 November 1786, 1 November 1787 and 13 December 1788.

12. McCord, N. *N.E. England: The Region's Development 1760–1960* (Batsford, 1979), p.37.

13. Durham Record Office (DRO), DU 1/12/33, 2/5/6, 2/1/5, 2/5/7, 2/5/9, Minute books and accounts of Durham Paving Commissioners.

14. DRO, DU 2/5/8.

15. DRO, DU 2/5/8.

16. DRO, DU 2/5/12.

17. DRO, DU 2/1/7.

18. According to Scoresby, whale oil was shipped in casks varying from 40–300 gallons; a cask was 35–40 gallons; a hogshead, 63 gallons; a pipe, 126 gallons; a tun, 252 gallons.

19. NRO, Morpeth Bailiff's Accounts, 1793–1835.

20. North Shields Local Studies Library (NSLS), 103/595. A handbill addressed to the inhabitants of North Shields.

21. Falkus, M.E. 'The British Gas Industry before 1850', *Economic History Review*, XX, (1967), pp.494–508.

22. Rees, A. *Manufacturing Industry (1819–20)*, Vol.4. A selection from *Universal Dictionary of Arts, Sciences and Literature* (David & Charles), p.51.

23. As late as 1837, Newcastle newspapers carried advertisements addressed to stock farmers which included the sale of whale oil with other commodities. See, for example, *Northern Liberator*, 28 October 1837.

24. *Newcastle Journal*, 3 April 1773.

25. *Newcastle Journal*, 3 November 1759.

26. Jones, S. 'A Maritime History of the Port of Whitby, 1714–1914', University of London, Ph.D. (1982), Chap. 5, Table 7.

27. Whitby ships regularly supplied whale oil to Sunderland, Scarborough and Stockton. See, for example, *Newcastle Advertiser*, 15 February 1806 or *Newcastle Chronicle*, 11 October 1817.

28. Barrow, A. 'Whale Fishery', University of Northumbria, Ph.D (1989), Part I, Chapter 4, Table 10.1.

29. NRO, Blackett (Wylam). Account book of the ship *Disko Bay*. Whalebone was shipped to Hamburg in 1785 and 1786 and entries for 18 December 1789 and 9 February 1790 refer to shipments of 'oyle to Rotterdam'.

30. Clitheroe, G. *The Ancient Mariners of Pickering* (Beck Isle Museum, Pickering, 1976).

31. NRO, ZAN M14/E16.

32. Stamp, T & C. *Greenland Voyager*, (Caedmon of Whitby), p.33.

33. *Newcastle Courant*, 19 October 1838.

34. NSLS. A handbill addressed to the inhabitants of North Shields, 1820.

6

'More wild and uncouth, more rough and blasphemous, more swayed by superstition than any other seamen under the British flag'

[B. Lubbock]

The Greenlandmen

The development of a whaling tradition amongst the merchant seamen of north-east England is, paradoxically, the best known and the least known aspect of the maritime heritage of the region. Whitby's association with the Greenland trade is, thanks to Scoresby, well established, but the whalermen of Sunderland, Shields and Berwick have gone largely unrecorded. These Greenlandmen or Greenlanders as they were known to their nautical contemporaries, were a hardy bunch, well used to the freezing temperatures and tempestuous weather conditions of the Arctic. They were renowned for their toughness, initiative and independence of spirit. Greenlandmen were feared as well as admired and many of them achieved a kind of folk hero status within the communities in which they lived. Andrew Shewan, the master of a China clipper, recalled shipping a crew at Peterhead in 1860 that had recently returned from a whaling voyage. Shewan warned the mates that these Greenland seamen had:

> *'...a freedom and truculence of demeanour not often encountered aboard the clipper ships...[they were]...little versed in the niceties of sea discipline and apt to consider that Jack was as good as his master.'* [1]

Who could command men such as these?

Hunting whales from open boats in sub-zero temperatures with primitive, hand-held harpoons demanded special skills and a particular kind of courage. Few other seaborne, maritime occupations in the days of sail demanded as much physical and mental endurance. An Arctic whaling voyage was not a venture for the faint hearted and few general seaman persevered with it:

> '...*I did not like the whale fishing*', recalled John Nichol in 1822, '*there is no sight for the eye of the inquisitive after the first glance and no variety to charm the mind...desolation reigns around, nothing but snow or bare rocks and ice. The cold is so intense and the weather often so thick...that I resolved to bid adieu to the coast of Greenland forever.*' [2]

Life on board the whaling ships was hard and uncompromising, living accommodation cramped and overcrowded. Large whalers like *Esk* or *Lord Gambier* carried seven whaleboats and crews of 45–50 men, manning levels far in excess of those that were usual in vessels of a similar size engaged in general trading. Even the whalers themselves carried fewer seamen for their voyages in the coal trade or out to the Baltic.[3] The experience of repeated voyages under the difficult and dangerous circumstances of Arctic sailing made the Greenlandmen entirely different to other classes of seafarers. Many of them were recruited from small fishing communities in Northumberland and north Yorkshire where particular families often provided skilled whalermen for generations. Others came from farming backgrounds or drifted into whaling for the adventure, the pay and the special privileges it provided them. Whatever the reason, successful whaling voyages depended upon their skills and experience and many of them spent their entire working lives at sea in Greenland ships. John Patterson, for example, born at North Shields in 1805, went to sea as a nine-year old cabin boy in 1814. He subsequently served in responsible positions on several Arctic whalers sailing from Shields and Whitby and eventually commanded ships at Hull, Shields and Aberdeen. When he retired from the sea in 1864 Patterson had completed 50 consecutive voyages to the Arctic.

During the Napoleonic War and just after there were over a thousand Greenlanders like Patterson based in the ports of north-east England. The whalers of Shields, Whitby and Berwick employed about half of them, the others sailed as harpooners, boatsteerers, cooks or sailmakers in the ships of other ports. Few vessels in the Hull whaling fleet sailed without crewmen from north-east England.[4] In the same way the ships of Aberdeen and Peterhead had a long tradition of employing whalermen from Shields and Whitby. The best known whaling family of any British port, the Grays of Peterhead, originated in South Shields, where the father of the dynasty, David Gray (1775–1833) had first mustered to a Tyne whaler, probably *Middleton*, in 1801.

At the end of the Napoleonic War in 1815 the British whaling fleet continued to sail for two distinct whaling grounds. Most of the Whitby fleet sailed to the Greenland grounds and, despite a steady decline in the size of whales regularly taken there, continued to prosper from their enterprise. Whale oil imports at Whitby exceeded 1,000 tuns almost every other year between 1814 and 1821 and individual ships often arrived with bumper cargoes. Despite his reputation as one of the great whale hunters, Scoresby's catches were regularly matched or exceeded by other Whitby captains like Kearsley of *Henrietta* and Johnson of *Aimwell*.

The whaleships of Newcastle and Berwick generally divided their effort between Greenland and the Davis Straits. Captains such as George Palmer of *Cove* and James Fleming of *Lady Jane* were amongst the first to exploit the Baffin Bay Fishery after its discovery in 1817. Within a few years all of the Newcastle ships were sailing there, despite the risks that it involved. The passage across Melville Bay to the so-called 'West water' was fraught with danger. Voyages lasted longer, ships sustained loss or damage more frequently and ice conditions played a crucial part in the success or failure of the annual fishery. Ten vessels were wrecked in Baffin Bay in 1819 and fourteen were wrecked there in 1821 although, remarkably, no local ships were lost on these occasions.

Arctic whalers usually left their home ports in February or March in order to reach the whaling grounds by the beginning of May. The Greenland Fishery generally lasted four or five months depending upon ice conditions and the difficulty of finding and pursuing the migrating whales. Voyages to the Davis Straits and Baffin Bay rarely lasted less than six months. The habit of calling at Orkney or Shetland to make up the crew and take on fresh water and provisions was well established by the end of the eighteenth century. The outward passage to the whaling grounds from Lerwick or Stromness usually took about a month and ships were frequently damaged confronting spring gales in the North Atlantic. In 1803 *Oak* of Whitby, Captain Banks, was severely damaged by a mountainous wave a few days after rounding Cape Farewell. The sea carried away *Oak*'s masts, bowsprit, rudder and all of her whaleboats. When the gale subsided the crew rigged jury masts and a temporary rudder and '*...after infinite toil and peril arrived safely in the harbour of Whitby...*'.[5]

In 1822 *Norfolk* of Berwick lost her master Captain Stephens and three seamen overboard in similar circumstances. The mate was so severely injured by the incident that he abandoned the voyage and put back to Stromness.

As the whalers approached the ice edge a drop in temperature of 25°F in a single day was not uncommon:

> '*10 April 1815. Lat.74°66'N Long.10°14'E*
> *The fall of the thermometer was very considerable this day...the exceptional cold and forcible wind called forth all the anti-gelid habiliments of the crew in the most ridiculous form and the most tasteless arrangement imaginable. In addition to the usual articles of*

dress...are...displayed in great profusion large boots, mitts and upper jackets, sashes for the waist, comforters for the neck and immense cow-hair wigs for the head and ears, decorated with prodigious tails covering the shoulders and extending half way down the back. Some of the crew wear waterproof sealskin jackets, trousers and mitts, thus altogether forming one of the most grotesque groups that can readily be imagined.' [6]

Little wonder Scoresby thought that there was '...*something ludicrous in the costume of a Greenland sailor*'![7] Once the ship reached the pack ice they were likely to find migrating whales and much of the hunting from this point was undertaken by the crews of whaleboats. Most whalers carried six or seven whaleboats, sleek, usually double-ended, carvel-built boats between 24-28 feet long. Each harpooner had his own boat and crew, drawn by lots on the outward voyage. In a trade surrounded by custom and superstition, a random method of selecting the personnel of each whaleboat had great significance for the men. In an enclosed community such as that of an Arctic whaler, it was extremely important that the crew should not suspect their officers of exhibiting favouritism when allocating the crew to their various tasks. The wages of the men ultimately depended upon the success of each whale- boat. If the talent and skills of individual harpooners and boatsteerers were unfairly distributed by the deliberate choice of the captain, the inevitable result would be resentment and discontent.[8]

Each whaleboat, distinctively painted in the colours of the parent ship, was equipped with several harpoons, four lances and five lengths of whale lines consisting of 120 fathoms of 2½ inch hemp neatly coiled in the bottom of the boat.[9] There were three key men in each whaleboat: the line manager who pulled stroke oar and took responsibility for coiling and attaching the whale-lines to the harpoons; the boatsteerer, who manœvred the whaleboat at the instructions of the harpooner and took responsibility for maintaining the equilibrium of the boat after the harpoon had struck the whale, and the harpooner, who was the most experienced man in the whaleboat and rowed bow oar. Since hand-held harpoons were only effective at eight to ten yards, the whaleboats stalked the slow moving leviathans from behind and to one side. The dangers associated with these close encounters were well known to the men. It was common for whaleboats to be overturned or smashed and for crew members to be killed or seriously injured. More often than not the chase ended in disappointment as the whales fled for the pack ice or harpoons drew. In 1828 *Cove* of South Shields, Captain George Palmer, reached the ice edge on 27 April a month out from Stromness. Her whaleboats were launched and recovered a dozen times during the following three weeks before the first whale was successfully harpooned and killed on 24 May. In 1829, *Cove* reached the ice on 25 April but no boats were launched until 11 July, almost three months later.[10]

Whaleboats often spent many hours at sea in atrocious weather conditions and the crew normally carried sufficient food and water to enable them to survive several days absence from the ship. In July 1820, a boat's crew belonging to *Eliza* of North Shields, Captain John Boswell, in endeavouring to tow the parent ship clear of the ice in a calm, became separated by a heavy swell. They were fortunate to be picked up by another whaler who found them on the ice the following day. They were lucky, as any delay in returning to the ship frequently resulted in exposure and frostbite, the dreaded curse of the whaling trade. Missing digits of hands and feet was one of the more obvious ways of identifying a Greenlandman. In 1822 a boat's crew of the Hull whaler *Royal George* was caught in a storm and returned to the ship many hours later, drenched and frozen. The surgeon was subsequently obliged to amputate 35 fingers and toes![11]

Despite the use of new and improved types of harpoon, including gun-harpoons, it often took three or four hours to dispatch a whale and sometimes up to a day. Once harpooned, the Greenland whale usually sounded, sometimes to incredible depths and at great speed, taking with it the heavy ropes so carefully coiled in the bottom of the whaleboat. Scoresby describes how a whale struck near the edge of an ice-field, could run out all of the whale-lines in the space of ten minutes before help could arrive from other whaleboats in the vicinity:

> '*...To retard, therefore, as much as possible, the flight of the whale, it is usual for the harpooner who strikes it to cast one, two or more turns around a kind of post called a bollard which is fixed within ten to twelve inches of the stem of the boat for the purpose. Such is the friction of the line when running around the bollard that it frequently envelopes the harpooner in smoke and if the wood was not frequently wetted would probably set fire to the boat. During the capture of one whale a groove is sometimes cut in the bollard nearly an inch in depth.*' [12]

The strength of some whales was prodigious:

> '*On 8 June 1821 in Latitude 77° in the Greenland Sea, Captain Scoresby when in command of the* Baffin *[harpooned a whale] which, after running out 15 lines and dragging two boats and 15 men both in the water and over the ice, was killed. When the lines were got in it was found that the fish had been dragging under the water six lines and a boat belonging to the* Trafalgar *of Hull.*' [13]

Once the whale had been successfully caught and killed it was towed to the parent ship and secured alongside so that the process of flensing could begin. Greenland whalers always worked from the body of the whale with the aid of 'speck-tackles', a system of blocks and ropes stretched from a guy between the main and mizzen mast. The whole operation was supervised by the spectioneer, the principal harpooner. The blubber was cut from the carcass of the whale and, by rotating the body through 90° after each strip of blubber had been torn free by the 'speck-tackle', the whale carcass could be processed. The strips of blubber were cast into the waist of the ship where they were cut into large chunks and 'made-off' into casks for storage. It was cold, greasy, back-breaking work, and most surviving logbooks confirm the routine of work and incident common to the Arctic whalers. If a ship found itself amongst a school of whales it became the scene of constant and frantic activity that sometimes lasted 48 hours without respite, and the conditions imposed upon ships and men were endured only in the expectation of high wages, which constituted one of the principal sources of attraction for many seamen.

Wages in the whaling trade were fixed to the profitability of the voyage and the value of the catch. In the Southern Whale Fishery seamen generally received a fixed proportion of the net profit of the voyage. In the Northern Whale Fishery wages were dependent upon the gross catch and fluctuated between one season and the next. But averaged over several years, the wages of the Greenlandmen were much greater than those that they might expect to earn from voyages in other trades.

According to Scoresby, writing in 1820, harpooners received half a guinea 'striking money' and six shillings per tun of oil secured by the voyage. Boatsteerers, line managers and seamen received 1/6d 'oil money' in addition to their basic monthly allowance. For a cargo boiling down to 200 tuns of oil, a harpooner might expect to make £70 for a Greenland voyage and an able seamen £25. For the principal officers at least this was substantially more than they might earn in the coal trade or during a series of Baltic voyages.

Since seasonal catches at the whaling grounds were the basis of calculating the earnings of Greenlandmen there were wide variations in annual pay. John Winter, mate and harpooner of *Cove* earned £96 for his share in the capture of eighteen whales during the voyage of 1820. In 1821 he earned £77 but in 1822 only £33. Winter was due to collect almost £100 for his part in the successful voyage of 1823 but on 17 September, only a day from Stromness, he was swept off the cathead and drowned: '*...it was quite impossible to use any means for saving him as the ship was running rapidly before the wind and the sea was so high that a boat could not live.*'[14] Winter's widow received his wages together with additional contributions from the captain and crew as was the custom amongst merchant seamen.

The intense frustration and disappointment of a difficult and unproductive voyage

Table 17. Wages in the whaling trade. *Baffin*, 1820

Position	*Wages per month (£.s.d)*	*Total earnings (£.s.d)*
Mate	3-0-0	61-1-6
Surgeon	4-0-0	25-5-0
Carpenter	5-0-0	25-5-0
Harpooner	3-15-0	49-12-3
Carpenter's mate	4-0-0	17-12-9
Boatsteerer	3-15-0	57-19-10
Cook	4-0-0	16-1-8
Steward	2-15-0	10-2-11
Armourer	3-0-0	2-11-0
Landsman	2-5-0	5-1-3
Able seaman	3-10-0	12-10-0
Seaman	2-0-0	4-16-3

Source The wages include 'oil money' at 1/6d per tun. Scoresby Archive, WLPS.
Notes:
(i) It is not clear how the low amounts recorded for the armourer, seaman and landsman has been calculated, and whether 'hand money' i.e. payment in advance to the dependants of the seamen had been deducted.
(ii) Harpooners were normally paid more than boatsteerers and a reversal of their respective earnings might seem more appropriate.
(iii) A footnote to the original table indicates that harpooners were paid £11-11-00 'fish striking money' for the 1820 voyage indicating that the vessel had secured 22 whales.

to the Davis Straits can only be imagined, and the frequency of such voyages increased after 1830. A public subscription for the relief of seamen employed in the Northern Whale Fishery was opened at Newcastle in October 1830, after the magnitude of the losses sustained in that year came to be appreciated.

> *'The situation of the seamen of the port of Newcastle-upon-Tyne employed in the Northern Whale Fishery is submitted to the consideration of the public; many of them who have been employed in the ships of other ports have suffered shipwreck and have returned home utterly destitute; whilst those who have been employed in the vessels belonging to their own port, though they have escaped the calamity of shipwreck, yet from the entire failure of the Fishery, on which their remuneration depends, are scarcely in a less necessitous condition.'* [15]

More than £500 was subsequently raised and distributed to the whalermen and their dependants. By contrast, in 1832, the Tyne whalers killed 126 whales yielding more

Table 18. Wages per month and bonus payments paid to the crew of *Lady Jane*, 1846-1848 (in £.s.d)

Position	*Payments*	*1846*	*1847*	*1848*
Mate	Sea pay	2-0-0	4-10-0	2-0-0
	Fish money	1-1-0	1-1-0	1-1-0
	Oil money	7-2	7-2	7-2
Surgeon	Sea pay	3-3-0	3-3-0	3-3-0
	Fish money	1-1-0	1-1-0	1-1-0
Carpenter	Sea pay	4-10-0	4-10-0	4-10-0
	Fish money	-	-	1-1-0
	Oil money	1-9	1-9	1-9
Harpooner	Sea pay	1-0-0	1-0-0	1-0-0
	Fish money	10-6	10-6	10-6
	Oil money	7-2	7-2	7-2
Boatsteerer	Sea pay	2-10-0	2-10-0	2-10-0
	Oil money	1-9	1-9	1-9
Cooper	Sea pay	3-10-0	4-10-0	3-10-0
	Oil money	3-0	3-0	3-0
Cook	Sea pay	2-10-0	2-10-0	2-10-0
	Oil money	1-9	1-9	1-9
Seaman	Sea pay	2-0-0	2-0-0	2-0-0
	Oil money	1-3	1-3	1-3

Source: PRO, BT 98/1041, 1364 and 1709.

than 1,000 tuns of whale oil '...*probably the greatest quantity ever brought to this port in one season*.'[16] The four vessels had an average cargo of 31 whales and 260 tuns of oil. Translated into wages at 1820 rates, this represented almost £112 for a mate, between £90-100 for a harpooner and £45 for an able seaman.

The rapid decline in the number of vessels engaged in Arctic whaling after 1830, reduced employment prospects and left a surplus of experienced men. In 1830, there were perhaps 4,500 seamen engaged on board the 91 vessels that sailed to the Arctic in that year. By 1841, there were only nineteen vessels employing about 1,000 seamen. Competition for the limited number of responsible posts interrupted the promotional pattern of earlier years and forced men with experience as harpooners to accept subsidiary positions as boatsteerers, or line managers. Many seamen left the whaling trade altogether and fewer young men were attracted to it. Increased

Table 19. Wages in the whaling trade, *Lady Jane*, 1844 to 1848 (in £.s.d)

Position	*1844*	*1845*	*1846*	*1847*	*1848*
Mate	33-10-0	72-18-4	55-0-0	54-3-9	33-10-0
Surgeon	23-2-0	55-13-0	27-6-0	21-10-0	25-4-0
Carpenter	36-9-0	78-12-6	45-18-0	31-05-9	36-9-0
Harpooner	27-10-0	66-18-4	49-0-0	14-19-2	27-10-0
Boatsteerer	20-5-0	29-17-6	25-10-0	17-03-9	20-5-0
Cooper	30-0-0	46-10-0	39-0-0	30-15-0	30-0-0
Cook	20-5-0	29-17-6	25-10-0	17-3-9	20-5-0
Seaman	15-15-0	22-2-6	19-10-0	13-11-3	15-15-0

Source: Barrow, A. 'North East Coast Whale Fishery, 1750-1850', University of Northumbria, Ph.D, Table 7.3, p.220.

Note:

(i) Wages for 1844 and 1845 are calculated on 1846 wage rates.

(ii) The success of the voyages was:

1844	4 whales	60 tuns oil
1845	35 whales	170 "
1846	8 whales	120 "
1847	2 whales	25 "
1848	4 whales	60 "

(iii) Harpooner's 'fish money' was paid to individual harpooners who struck whales and is not included in the calculation of their wages. It may have added £5 to each harpooner's income in 1845, but less than £1 in the other years. It is not clear how the surgeon and the carpenter were paid their 'fish money', and it has been assumed that they were paid according to the total number of whales secured by

competition amongst experienced whalermen, together with the declining productivity of their vessels, inevitably led to wage adjustments.

The poor seasons of 1835 to 1837 and 1839 to 1841 also drove wage rates down. Wages paid to the crew of *Lady Jane* between 1846 and 1848, indicates that monthly sea pay had fallen by 25–30 per cent compared to 1820, although bonus payments seem to have remained about the same, or even increased slightly. 'Oil money' paid to harpooners had increased from 6/- to 7/2d per tun, but monthly sea pay had fallen to £1 per month, the lowest rate paid to any member of the crew. The monthly rates for the mate, the surgeon, the carpenter, the cook and the boatsteeers had also fallen, although their bonus payments remained about the same. Such wage adjustments reflected the owners' response to the decline in the average catch of most whalers after 1835.

When George Harrison was the master of *Lady Jane*, between 1838 and 1847, he had two very successful seasons, in 1838 and 1845, when the crew killed 23 and 35 whales respectively. But in 1840, only one whale was killed, and in 1841 the vessel returned 'clean' from the whaling grounds. The average catch of *Lady Jane* between 1838 and 1847 was ten whales and about 88 tuns of oil. Given these seasonal fluctuations, earnings varied enormously (see Tables 18 and 19).

Of course, potential earnings was not the only attraction of a Greenland voyage, particularly during the eighteenth century. Before 1815 seamen enlisting with a Greenland whaler were given a protection from impressment for the duration of the voyage. Harpooners, boatsteerers and line managers retained their protection certificates during the winter months, when the vessel was engaged in other trades. Ordinary seamen were obliged to have them renewed at the beginning of each year. These protection certificates had a real value for the men and their improper use was common. At Sunderland, forged protections were sold for 8/6d each, and could fetch as much as £3 in London.[17] A protected man who stretched his protection too far, like the Greenland harpooner found on his way to Ostend,[18] was in for trouble, and in times of crisis, particularly during wartime, the Admiralty were apt to ignore them. The heavy manning levels of Greenland ships made them prime targets for the Navy and seamen were resentful of the regular appearance of naval press-gangs. In August 1756, 40 Greenland seamen, probably the nucleus of the crews of the Newcastle Whaling Company's ships, arrived outside the Custom House on the Quayside at Newcastle seeking to renew their protections. Two naval lieutenants with attendant gangs sought to impress the men and a violent running fight ensued:

> *'...one of the lieutenants, being hard-pressed, drew his sword and ran one of the Greenlanders through his hand, but the wounded man nevertheless, getting his sword from him, in return cut out his eye and part of his cheek and gave him a stab in the thigh.'*[19]

The fight broke up when the press-gang received orders to withdraw. Such concerted opposition was not as effective when naval frigates sought to impress Greenlanders while they were still at sea. Warships often boarded whalers on their return voyages from the Orkneys, particularly off St. Abb's Head or the Farne Islands. It became the practice of the crews of some whalers to leave the ship off the Northumberland coast, and return to Tyneside on foot, rather than risk a confrontation with the Navy off Tynemouth. The crew of *Kitty* are reported to have done this in 1779.[20]

Whitby ships would sometimes discharge their crews in Teesmouth if a 'hot press' was known to be taking place. Impressment of Greenlandmen at sea was common during the French Wars. In 1804, thirteen of the crew of *Henrietta* were impressed by *Princess of Wales*, cutter, and in 1806 a dozen of the crew of *John and Margaret* of Shields were impressed by *Druid*, frigate. Ironically, *Druid* had been sent to protect the whaling fleet from the activities of French privateers. Most of the pressed men were relatively inexperienced Greenland hands who were eventually persuaded to muster as volunteers, entitling them to the usual bounty payments.[21] Organized resistance of merchant seamen on shore made the task of the press-gangs more difficult. Greenlandmen were often at the centre of this resistance and they made a positive contribution to the development of trade unionism amongst the seamen of north-east England.

Because of the special circumstances in which they worked, their protected status and earning power, the whalermen commanded great respect in their maritime communities and their role in the organisation and leadership of the merchant seamen in the coal trade was well known to the authorities. In his evidence to a Parliamentary Select Committee in 1800, a local shipowner was asked:

> '...*Are the men under Greenland protections the principal movers in all instances when the coal ships are detained in the Tyne and Wear?*'

He answered:

> '*They are the ringleaders of all the disturbances for raising wages. There are hardly any instances of detention but when the Greenlanders are in port.*'[22]

Merchant seamen engaged in the coal trade displayed considerable cohesion and were well aware of their capacity to exploit the vulnerability of the coal and shipping interests to stoppages in the trade, particularly in late summer. The combined effect of re-employment of returning whaleships in the coal trade and the reintegration of the Greenlanders amongst the collier seamen created the conditions in which trade disputes occurred. Since the whalermen were well paid by comparison to the collier seamen, the disparity in their relative earnings during the winter months often triggered wage disputes. Moreover, it was not uncommon for shipowners to provoke strikes by reducing wage rates on the arrival of the Greenland ships because their crews created a temporary surplus in the labour market.[23] The seamen's strikes of 1792, 1806 and 1815 were directly related to the arrival of the Greenland ships and the leaders of the strike committees usually included whalermen.

The strike of 1792 originated in an atmosphere of rising prices and was based on the seamen's demand for an increase in wages to £3 per voyage during the winter months. The seamen enforced their demand by stopping the coal trade and removing crews from all ships then lying in Tyne harbour. The crews of ships newly arriving in the Tyne quickly became involved as well. Another trigger of the 1792 strike had been the disastrous whaling season of that year. Half of the Tyne whaling fleet had returned 'clean', so had three whaleships at Sunderland, and the Whitby ships fared badly too. The intense disappointment and frustration of these unproductive voyages left the Greenlandmen and their families with an insufficient income and forced them to rely upon their winter earnings in the coal trade. They clearly had a vested interest in the success of the strike. In October 1806 the Newcastle newspapers reported the outbreak of fresh disturbances amongst the merchant seamen at Shields:

> '...*As usual at this season a number of loose young men with Greenland protections from the impress assemble at this town, North and South Shields demanding and extorting such and such sums for a voyage in the coal trade, which, if not granted...they stop the ships from proceeding.*' [24]

The strike of 1806 stopped the coal trade for two weeks before: '...*the turbulent Greenlanders at Shields [were] suppressed by the vigilance of the magistracy aided by H.M. troops.*'[25]

The clearest evidence for the role of the whalermen in the instigation and management of seamen's strikes on the river Tyne relates to the famous strike of 1815. The strike had a number of causes principally related to the employment of foreign seamen when many British mariners were unemployed, the undermanning of colliers and the shipowners' proposals for wage reductions. The first hints of trouble were reported soon after the arrival of the Greenland ships, and no colliers sailed from the Tyne between 4 September and 22 October 1815.

The correspondence between Captain Caulfield, the Regulating Captain at North Shields and the Admiralty, represents one of the principal sources of information about the 1815 strike and provides some fascinating insights into the circumstances of the dispute. In one of his earliest letters Caulfield observed: '...*I now learn that the Greenland seamen have been the chief promoters in the present proceedings.*'[26] The signatures contained in the Seamen's Petition leave little doubt that Caulfield was correct in his assertion. It contains the names of numerous whalermen who are known to have sailed in the ships of Shields, Whitby and Hull. Amongst the first names on the petition were Daniel McFarland, a member of the strike committee, and Samuel

Brown, a young harpooner. The distinctive names of Cumberland Adamson, William Beautyman, Miles Burkitt, a Gateshead man and Ephrahim Turpin from Cullercoats represent a few of the many examples of the Greenland seamen who were involved in the 1815 strike.[27] In reporting the end of the strike in October, the Newcastle newspapers were in no doubt who was to blame:

> '*...on deeply investigating into the system which springs from the spirit of resistance to regular authority...not one of the many turbulent sailors apprehended had been on board a man-of-war, but consisted chiefly of Greenlandmen and runaway apprentices of profligate morals...*' [28]

With an allowance for the less than objective tone of the newspaper report, it is clear that the importance of the Greenlandmen was acknowledged by many contemporary observers of the 1815 strike and confirmed by the muster books of numerous whaleships. But the 1815 dispute represented the last occasion when Greenland seamen were sufficiently numerous in the ports of north-east England for them to influence the course of events.

Arctic whaling went into serious decline after 1820. The combination of longer voyages and fewer ships, with a rapid expansion of the collier fleet eroded the influence the Greenlandmen had once enjoyed. Many of them were absorbed into general trading and those who remained were obliged to accept lower basic rates of pay and less attractive bonus payments. Many local whalermen lost their lives during the Arctic tragedies of 1835-36 and 1836-37, when a number of whaleships were forced to winter in the Davis Straits without sufficient food or clothing to survive the experience. Some of these men had signed the Seamen's Petition in 1815. Thomas Robinson, mate of *Lady Jane* and John Dodds, harpooner, both died in that ship in 1836.[29] Thomas Hall, a Tweedmouth man mustered as a harpooner of *Norfolk*, died of scurvy in March 1837.[30] Samuel Brown was employed as the cook of *Dee* of Aberdeen at the time of his death in 1837, Miles Burkitt, the cook of *Lady Jane*, survived the experience.[31]

These men were amongst the last of several generations of Greenlandmen who manned the ships of Britain's Arctic whaling fleet. A century after the 1815 strike, the death of the last of the old Greenland hands of North Shields, James Thompson, aged 91, was considered sufficiently noteworthy to warrant an extensive obituary in the Newcastle papers.[32] The impact of Greenland whalermen like Thompson, upon the maritime communities in which they lived clearly survived long after the whaling trade ceased to have any importance.

References

1. Clarke, J.V. *The Last of the Whaling Captains* (Brown, Son and Ferguson, 1986), p.172.

2. Nichol spent most of his career as a cooper on various men-of-war. He undertook a single whaling voyage on *Leviathan* of London in 1784. His reminiscence was recorded by a local bookseller in Edinburgh when Nichol was an old man and begging in the streets of his home town. It was published as *Life and Adventures of John Nichol, Mariner* (Blackwood, Edinburgh), 1822.

3. For example, in 1771 *Royal Exchange* of Newcastle mustered 42 seamen for a Greenland voyage but regularly employed just fifteen men during four voyages in the coal trade between May 1771 and April 1772. Public Record Office (PRO), BT 98/125 No.169.

4. In 1789 the master of *Elizabeth*, Thomas Nellis, lived in Sandsend and six of the seven harpooners came from Whitby. Other crew members had previously served in Whitby whalers, Hull Trinity House (HTH), Muster Roll of *Elizabeth*, No. 104, 1789. Similarly, the Muster Roll of *Harmony* in 1814, reveals that both of the mates, the carpenters and two each of the harpooners, boatsteerers and line managers came from Shields, HTH, Muster Roll of *Harmony*, No. 2, 1814.

5. *Newcastle Courant*, 23 July 1803.

6. Scoresby, W. 'Journals of the *Esk*', quoted in Stamp, T. & C. *Greenland Voyager* (Caedmon of Whitby), pp.18-19.

7. Scoresby, W. 'Journals of the *Esk*', p.19.

8. An account of the practice of selecting whaleboats and crews can be found in Credland, A.G. (Ed), *The Journal of Surgeon Cass Aboard the Whaler* Brunswick *of Hull, 1824* (Humberside Heritage Publications), No.18, Humberside Libraries and Arts (1988).

9. Bickerdyke, J. *Sea Fishing* (Longmans, Green and Co, 1895), p.480.

10. Logbook of the whaler *Cove* of South Shields, Captain George Palmer. Entries for April–May 1828 and April–July 1829, George Palmer Collection, Southwold.

11. Breummer, F. *Life of the Harp Seal* (David and Charles, 1978), p.122.

12. Scoresby, W. *Arctic Regions*, II, p.245.

13. Lubbock, B. *The Arctic Whalers* (Brown, Son and Ferguson, 1937), p.19.

14. Logbook of *Cove*, Captain George Palmer, 17 September 1823.

15. *Newcastle Courant*, 20 November 1830.

16. *Newcastle Chronicle*, 27 October 1832.

17. Lloyd, C. *The British Seaman* (Collins, 1968), p.163.

18. Lloyd, C. *British Seamen*, p.163.

19. *Newcastle Intelligencer*, 11 August 1756.

20. *Newcastle Journal*, 3 July 1779.

21. PRO, ADM 51/1608 and ADM 36/17072, Logbook and Muster book of *H.M.S Druid*. Five of the men impressed were line managers and the others able seamen.

22. Select Committee on the Coal Trade, British Parliamentary Papers (BPP), x646 (1800). Evidence of William Marshall.

23. The Liverpool Riots of 1775 were provoked in this way and it was undoubtedly a factor in the seamen's strike on the river Tyne in 1815.

24. *Newcastle Courant*, 25 October 1806.

25. *Newcastle Courant*, 1 November 1806.

26. PRO, ADM 1/1669. Captain Caulfield to Secretary of the Admiralty, 10 September 1815.

27. The various muster rolls and crew lists of whalers at Shields, Berwick, Whitby and Hull reveal many more names. Adamson was an old Greenland hand who had served on *John and Margaret* during the 1780s (see, for example, PRO,

BT 98/129 No. 212 or PRO, BT 98/130, No. 88). William Beautyman was then serving as the mate of the Tyne whaler *British Queen*, commanded by his brother Cuthbert. Miles Burkitt was serving as a harpooner on *Cove* and is mentioned on numerous occasions in the *Cove* logbooks. Ephrahim Turpin was a harpooner on *Ingria*, a Hull whaler (see HTH, Muster roll of *Ingria*, No. 184, 1815). He later commanded whaleships at Hull, Leith, Whitby and London before his whaling career ended in shipwreck in 1836.

28. *Newcastle Courant*, 28 October 1815.

29. *Newcastle Chronicle*, 21 March 1836.

30. PRO, BT 98/174, Crew List of *Norfolk* of Berwick.

31. PRO, BT 98/141 and BT 98/420, Crew Lists of *Dee* of Aberdeen and *Lady Jane* of Newcastle.

32. *Newcastle Daily Chronicle*, 26 February 1915.

7

'...the ice is fast around us and nothing to be seen but a solid plain as far as the eye can reach...'

[A seaman on board *Grenville Bay*, 31 December 1836]

Shipwreck, Disaster and Decline, 1820-1842

Whitby, 1820-1837

When Scoresby's comprehensive *Arctic Regions* was published in 1820 there was little indication that British whaling stood at the threshold of a terminal decline. He wrote during a period of post-war prosperity in the whaling trade when average catches were good, oil prices high and the industry generally buoyant. Scoresby undoubtedly saw, but failed to stress, a number of emerging threats to the long-term prosperity of Arctic enterprise; free trade, commodity substitution and increasing difficulties encountered by the whalers themselves.[1] Despite the discovery of the Baffin Bay Fishery in 1817 the emphasis of British whaling effort before 1821 remained within the older Greenland grounds. The Scoresbys and the majority of their contemporaries at Whitby and elsewhere sailed exclusively to the Greenland Sea throughout their careers. Indeed, Whitby ships specialized in the Greenland Fishery to such an extent that the entire fleet sailed there in 1819 and 1820.[2] But a combination of fewer whales, reduced oil prices and unpredictable weather conditions presented local whaler owners with a mounting dilemma. Scoresby alluded to the disparity in size between the whales then being taken on the Greenland grounds compared to the larger animals being killed by fewer vessels in the Davis Straits.[3] It meant that Greenland ships needed to procure more whales to achieve a comparable cargo and few of them were able to do so on a regular basis. Those that did were often obliged to stay out longer on the grounds which in turn compromised opportunities to undertake late season voyages in general trade. The importance of combining coal, Baltic and whaling voyages by the same ship in a single year can hardly be underestimated. It was one of the principal attractions of the Greenland Fishery for many shipowners, particularly at Whitby which had little internal trade of its own.

As the events of 1819-1822 gradually unfolded whaler owners everywhere faced some stark choices. Some of them switched their ships to longer, more expensive and potentially more damaging voyages to the Davis Straits and Baffin Bay in a quest for greater productivity. Others withdrew their ships altogether or reduced the size of their fleet by persevering only with those ships that had made a speciality of sailing to the Davis Straits. The majority of owners at Whitby doggedly persevered with voyages to Greenland in the hope that fewer ships sailing there would increase the productivity of those which remained. It was a strategy that seemed to work, in the short term at least. At a time when the British whaling fleet declined by 30 per cent between 1820 and 1825 and the proportion of ships sailing to Greenland by a staggering 80 per cent,[4] Whitby continued to send the same number of ships to the Arctic. Remarkably, the shipwrecks of 1819-1822 affected Whitby less than it did other ports. After more than 40 years the old *Henrietta* was sold to Aberdeen in 1820 and *Valiant* was lost at the Davis Straits in 1822. But no ships were deliberately withdrawn from the trade and Whitby still had a fleet of ten whalers in 1824. Chance and misfortune rather than economics seems to have played a greater role in the decline of whaling from the river Esk during the following years. The first to go was *Aimwell* wrecked at the Greenland Fishery in 1824. She struck a large piece of floe ice which stove the port bow so severely that she quickly filled with water and sank. In 1825 three of the Whitby ships returned 'clean' and the remainder of the fleet, with the exception of *Phoenix*, had poor catches. Even these reverses could hardly have prepared the port for the double tragedy of 1826.

It began with the loss of *Lively*, wrecked off the coast of eastern Greenland in May; there were no survivors. It ended with one of the most notorious shipwrecks ever to occur off the Yorkshire coast. On 6 September 1826, *Esk* was within 30 miles of Whitby but making slow progress against a freshening southerly breeze. As evening drew on she shortened sail and moved closer inshore to gain the benefit of a south-flowing flood tide across Tees Bay. It was a fateful decision. Within hours a violent easterly gale caught *Esk* on a lee shore. Despite the frantic efforts of an experienced crew she grounded on the Saltscar reef between Redcar and Marske where she was pounded mercilessly by enormous waves. The crew of Redcar lifeboat made several unsuccessful attempts to reach the wreck and rescue the crew. In the grey light of dawn *Esk* finally broke up and her crew pitched into the sea. There were only three survivors. Whitby whaling never really recovered from the tragedy. The loss of *William and Ann* in 1830 temporarily reduced the Whitby whaling fleet to a single ship.[5]

The whaling season of 1830 was notorious in the Arctic Fishery. *William and Ann* was one of nineteen vessels shipwrecked that year. Scoresby's old ship, *Baffin*, now whaling from Leith, was another. The destruction of *William and Ann* was witnessed by the crew of *Eagle* of Hull who received fourteen of the Whitby men on board including Captain Terry.[6] Further south the remaining Whitby ship, *Pheonix*, was badly damaged. Close by, *Cove* of Newcastle witnessed the destruction of five whalers within a quarter of a mile of her own position. *Phoenix* and *Cove* remained locked in the pack ice for almost a month before they eventually forced a passage into Baffin Bay at the end of August. But even then, their ordeal was far from over; the Arctic reserved one of its most violent storms for the departure of the surviving ships. *Eagle*, with the Whitby men still on board, was battered by mountainous seas and forced to heave-to under a mizzen staysail. George Palmer, master of *Cove*, considered the storm of 12 October 1830 so violent that '*...no former year could be referred to for an example*'. *Cove*'s logbook recorded:

> '*...Weather remarkably boisterous and thick with snow not being able to see more than 2 ships lengths. Consequently no exertion or judgement used by us could have availed in securing us from destruction that seemed inevitable because the icebergs were innumerable around.*'[7]

Whitby's lone whaler, *Phoenix*, limped into port at the end of October 1830 with the produce of four whales; it was a commendable performance given the circumstances of a disastrous season. Over the years, *Phoenix* had become the most consistently successful whaler in the Whitby fleet. Built and owned by the Chapman family and introduced to the Greenland trade as a new ship in 1816, she was one of the vessels whose switch from Greenland to Davis Straits voyages proved to be an immediate success. *Phoenix* obtained as much oil during two voyages in 1823-1824 as she had in seven previous voyages to the Greenland grounds. Thereafter, first under Captain Hallilee and then Captain Mills, *Phoenix* matched or exceeded the seasonal catches of every other Whitby whaler until 1835. In twelve voyages between 1823 and 1834 *Phoenix* earned profits in excess of £20,000 for the Chapman family and performed only one loss-making voyage, in 1831. Even this was more than offset by the bumper catch of the following year. In 1832, *Phoenix* brought into Whitby 235 tuns of oil, the largest quantity ever imported by one vessel in a single year. The total value of the cargo, including the whalebone, amounted to more than £7,000. Such was the optimism of the Chapman family that they placed a second ship, *Camden*, into the whaling trade from 1833. Built at Whitby in 1813, she was one of the largest whalers ever to sail from the port. Her master, John Armstrong, was an experienced whalerman from Cullercoats; the mate (after 1834) was John Patterson of North Shields.[8] *Camden*'s maiden whaling voyage was a great success, but subsequent seasons, with the exception of 1835, were poor.

Despite the efforts of an experienced crew, *Camden* returned 'clean' in 1836 and 1837. She was withdrawn from whaling after five voyages. *Phoenix* ended her whaling career under different circumstances. On 6 April 1837 as she was towed to sea by *Streonsahl*, steam tug, *Phoenix* broke adrift and drove ashore on the scar behind the East Pier where she lay stranded for two weeks. She was eventually refloated, repaired and sold to owners at Scarborough who employed her in the timber trade for many years. Whitby's long association with Arctic whaling had come to an end.

Newcastle, 1820-1842

The collapse of Greenland whaling initially affected Newcastle more than it did Whitby. A fleet of six ships in 1821 was reduced to three by 1823. *James* was the first to suffer, wrecked off Aberdeen on her maiden whaling voyage in 1821, less than 24 hours after sailing from the river Tyne. Then *Eliza* and *British Queen* were wrecked in Baffin Bay in 1822. Despite these reverses other Newcastle owners persevered. The experience of the Chapman family at Whitby demonstrated that the financial rewards of a successful voyage to the Arctic more than outweighed the physical risks that it often involved and *Phoenix* was not unique in her success. Whalers sailing from the river Tyne between 1823-1829 individually obtained between 80-280 tuns of whale oil per season. In 1825 *Lady Jane* earned over £9,000 for her owners and *Cove* more than £8,000 in 1829. *Grenville Bay*, the third ship of the Newcastle fleet, appears to have earned a cumulative profit of £19,000 in seven voyages during those years.[9] It was the most successful phase of the Davis Straits Whale Fishery.[10]

By 1830 the whaling trade at Newcastle was dominated by a single businessman, Thomas Richard Batson. Batson was a banker, shipowner and general merchant with extensive commercial interests at Berwick and on Tyneside. He was a partner in the Tweed Bank and later, in 1832, elected as the managing director of the North of England Joint Stock Bank. He became an alderman of Newcastle in 1835. Batson's shipowning interests were dominated by whaling vessels. By 1831 he was the sole owner of two large Tyne whalers, *Grenville Bay* (340 tons) and *Lord Gambier* (407 tons), had an eighth share in *Lady Jane* also of Newcastle and a similar interest in *Norfolk* of Berwick through his association with the Tweed Bank. Batson's singular interest in whaling ships contributed significantly to his reputation as one of Tyneside's foremost businessmen. Averaged over several seasons, Batson's whalers generated substantial annual incomes and he was fortunate that none of his ships were affected by the disasters of 1830. Given the increasingly unpredictable character of the Arctic Fishery it made sense to use the financial success of one ship to underwrite the failure of another. Before 1835 consecutive poor seasons on the whaling grounds were rare, and when they did occur, they were usually followed by exceptionally productive years. In 1830 and 1831, for example, the British whaling fleet killed 612 whales at an average of just under four whales per ship. In 1832 and 1833 a massive 3,258 whales were taken by fewer ships at an average of over 22 whales per ship.[11] Batson's whalers, like Chapman's at Whitby made enormous profits during these years. Thereafter, an unprecedented sequence of bad weather and poor seasons compromised the business security of both and precipitated their withdrawal from the trade.

In 1835-1837 the elements combined to produce the most catastrophic whaling seasons in the history of the British Whale Fishery. By this date whalers were penetrating into the waters of Baffin Bay, Lancaster Sound and Pond Inlet whenever ice conditions would allow. In these high northern latitudes of Arctic Canada the whalermen were pushing at the boundaries of sailing ship technology and they were ill-equipped to face the hazards that it involved. Seventy ships sailed to the Davis Straits in 1835, but in the unfavourable ice conditions several were wrecked and only about twenty managed to penetrate to the 'west water'. By early October, eleven of them were locked in the pack ice near Home Bay and Cape Dyer, between latitudes 69°20'N and 68°55'N. Amongst the trapped vessels were two of the Newcastle ships *Lady Jane* and *Grenville Bay* together with *Norfolk* of Berwick. They had entered the pack ice at the end of September in an attempt to find a passage to the south. The surgeon of *Lady Jane*, James Williamson (1814-1899) then a young South Shields doctor, subsequently recorded the experiences of the crew.[12]

The Ice-Drift Voyage of *Lady Jane*, 1835-1836

Lady Jane was the best known of all the Newcastle whalers. She had been built on the river Thames in 1772 and was originally introduced to the Whale Fishery at Hull in 1788. Transferred to Newcastle registry in 1804 she resumed her career as an Arctic whaler and spent the remainder of her working life in the trade. By 1835 her principal owners were Matthew Plummer & Co., one of Newcastle's leading merchant houses, with Thomas Richard Batson owning an eighth share in the ship. The master of *Lady Jane* was James Leask an Orkneyman from Stromness. Despite his relative inexperience as a captain (he had only been in command for two years), Leask had navigated *Lady Jane* as far as Sanderson's Hope on the western coast of Greenland by the beginning of July. Finding the pack ice impenetrable he turned to the south in search of a passage to the 'west water'. He found it, but *Lady Jane* was close beset in the land floe off Home Bay by the beginning of August. Active whaling was impossible even though some whales had been sighted. *Lady Jane*, together with the Hull whaler *Mary Frances* and several other ships, edged a few miles further north on 16 August before they were all forced to cut docks in the land floe. Williamson's Journal recorded the loss of the Hull ship a few days later:

> '*August 26 1835:*
> *At 3 a.m.* Mary Frances *lost. At 8 a.m. got the crew on board consisting of 53 men including the captain.*'

> '*August 28 1835:*
> *At 6 a.m. called all hands to secure provisions from the wreck. At 2 p.m. returned with two boat loads.*'

The crew of *Mary Frances* remained on board *Lady Jane* for two weeks before they were redistributed around other ships of the whaling fleet. Ten each went on board *Swan* and *Abram* on 11 September, nine more crossed to *Harmony* on 13 September, eight went to *Alfred* on 21 September and another six to *Duncombe* the following day. There was no indication at this stage of the complaints they subsequently made against the crew of *Lady Jane.*

It was late in the season and all of the ships had entered the pack ice in an attempt to force a passage to the south. All of their efforts were fruitless and in early October '*...it was judged necessary to place the ship's company on allowance of victuals...*'. [13]

There were seven other ships in the vicinity of *Lady Jane* at this time. One of them *Dordon* of Hull was lost close by on 20 October. The crew of *Lady Jane* spent the next ten days procuring fuel and provisions from the wreck. The remaining ships were then in 67°30'N. On 24 October, Thomas Taylor, master of another Newcastle ship *Grenville Bay*, wrote to Thomas Richard Batson:

> '*...I am sorry to have to write to you from this place. The winter has set in very soon and cold and we are frozen up in a floe drifting down the country...the ships are drifting down the straits about eight miles a day, and by the end of the month we will be clear of Cape Walsingham...I hope the ice will open south of that Cape.*' [14]

Taylor's prediction proved to be correct, although his escape took somewhat longer than he had anticipated. On 20 November the ships were near 64°N where they observed land 40 miles to the west. But the ships were beginning to move apart by this time and *Lady Jane* gradually became separated from the others. By 8 December they were in the mouth of Hudson Strait, within sight of Resolution Island, between fifteen and twenty miles to the east. The account continued:

> '...*they were then carried by the current to Green Island and proceeded a considerable way into Ungava Bay, where they were apprehensive that they would have to winter. In fact they bore up to endeavour to reach a settlement as a place of security and to obtain supplies. From the haziness of the weather they did not know with certainty where they were, but fortunately meeting with a strong current they were driven rapidly out of the strait, passing Button Island.*'[15]

Only two other ships remained in sight of *Lady Jane* by this date, *Norfolk* and *Grenville Bay*, and both disappeared to the south soon afterwards. More ominously, Williamson recorded the first death amongst the crew of *Lady Jane* on 10 December when William Oliver died of consumption; he was buried through the ice the following day. *Lady Jane* was then near 60°29'N. The other ships had broken free of the ice on 16 December 1835 in latitude 58°50'N, about 30 miles from the coast of Labrador. They had drifted almost 600 miles since the beginning of October. *Norfolk* and *Grenville Bay* arrived at their home ports of Berwick and Newcastle in early January 1836. The men were weak and a number of them exhibited signs of scurvy but none of them died of the disease. Surprisingly, only one fatality was recorded amongst the crews of these whalers during their eventful voyages.[16]

The crew of *Lady Jane* were not so fortunate. Drifting much closer to the coast than the other ships, *Lady Jane*'s southward progress was much slower, even though her observed position was already less than the latitude at which the other ships had escaped. On 20 December, Cape Chugford was twelve miles to the west, but the ship was frozen solidly in the floe. Williamson recorded the appearance of scurvy on 22 December. The crew was extremely weak and several of them had already taken to their beds: '...*being unprovided with sufficient clothing to defend against the severity of the weather which we thought daily becoming more intense*...'.[17]

The first death from scurvy occurred on 31 January 1836, when *Lady Jane* was in latitude 52°50'N and under heavy pressure from the ice. Conditions on board were graphically described by a survivor, George Francis:

> '...*The frost was that severe that it penetrated through the deck and the ships sides about two inches thick so that the bedclothes was frose* [sic] *fast to the sides of the ship and bed-cabin...when death had visited the poor souls their bodies were halled* [sic] *out of the bed-cabins and thrown overboard directly without being sewed up or putting into any form whatever to commit to the deep.*' [18]

Ten men succumbed to scurvy before *Lady Jane* eventually reached open water on 19 February 1836; the vessel was then at latitude 52°18'N and had drifted almost one thousand miles since the beginning of October. The death toll had reached 22 when *Lady Jane* arrived at Stromness on 12 March. Another five seamen were beyond recovery and died within days of their arrival in the makeshift hospital established by Captain James Clark Ross, R.N., who had commanded *Cove* in an attempt to relieve the trapped whalers.

> '*The appearance of the survivors and the distress of the friends of the dead*' reported one newspaper account, '*baffles all description. It drew tears from the eyes of many unconcerned spectators...such scenes Stromness never witnessed before.*' [19]

The loss of life fell particularly on the Orkneymen; thirteen of the twenty-three seamen who had mustered for *Lady Jane* at Stromness the year before, perished. Twelve hands were engaged to sail the vessel back to the river Tyne, where she arrived on 26 March. *Lady Jane* had then been twelve months and two weeks from Shields. Her voyage and those of the other ships raised public awareness and began a debate about conditions aboard Arctic whalers that rumbled on for several years. Recriminations followed the arrival of *Lady Jane* on Tyneside. A public inquiry was convened by Newcastle Trinity House to examine a series of accusations levelled at the master, James Leask, by six members of the crew. They challenged the substance of a number of reports that had circulated in local newspapers prior to their arrival from Stromness. These related to the burning of the wreck of *Mary Frances* in August 1835 and the competence of their captain. They emphatically denied any involvement in the destruction of the Hull ship, although Williamson's evidence admitted to: '*a little bit of a scruffage*' the crew insisted that '*the guilt must rest solely with that vessel's own crew...*'.[20]

Captain Leask was accused of misrepresenting the crew, failure to distribute provisions fairly, cruelty and incompetence. The charge concerning provisions and the evidence discussed in relation to it throws an interesting light on the seamens' perception of a healthy diet.

> '*We think that Captain Leask is deserving of great blame for not distributing liberally the provisions which the ship afforded, such as raisins, currants, rice and wine. These would have been of great service to the whole crew, but were not given even to those who were labouring under the severest illness.*' [21]

Leask's principal accuser was Henry Jameson, a boatsteerer, who was clearly aware of the anti-scorbutic qualities of these foodstuffs even though his information about the quantities on board was in error. Captain Leask denied that there had been any rice but admitted that he had taken out 56 pounds of raisins and the same quantity of currants but '*...they were for the use of the cabin and he considered it to be at the discretion* *of the master to give them out when he thought proper...'.*[22] Jameson claimed that the crew had only tasted them on Good Friday and Christmas Day and then only three quarts for 65 men. By contrast he saw the captain *'with his pockets full eating them upon the deck'.*[23] Williamson's evidence generally supported the captain's account and the Court of Enquiry subsequently exonerated Leask of all the charges brought against him. But the affair ended unsatisfactorily and with much bitterness. British whalers were obviously carrying anti-scorbutic foodstuffs as a luxury for the stern cabin rather than as a necessity for the men. It seems ironic that the Tyneside merchant community subsequently raised and distributed over £1,000 for the relief of the victims and their dependants[24] when they could have provided anti- scorbutics to all of the men for a fraction of this amount.

The provisioning of ships in the Northern Whale Fishery became the subject of considerable debate in the spring of 1836. It is clear, however, that few of the ships sent to the Arctic that year carried more than six months provisions and little in the way of anti-scorbutics, despite the experiences of the previous winter. There was some obvious concern on Tyneside:

> *'Now that the whalers are preparing to proceed on another voyage to the Davis Straits, we would beg to urge upon the attention of the owners the necessity of well provisioning their ships so as to guard against similar disasters to those which have so recently happened...and those who cannot afford a proper outfit should really not send their vessels to the Davis Straits. The custom at this port is to provision for nine months...a keel of coal is generally taken, but as fuel is of great importance and the expense not much, we would suggest that the quantity be increased to a keel and a half.'* [25]

The Ice Drifts of *Grenville Bay* and *Norfolk* 1836-37

Ice conditions in 1836-37 were little better than the year before and the whalers from north-east England found themselves trapped with four other ships abreast of Pond Inlet by the middle of September. George Harrison, master of *Norfolk*, believed his position to have been latitude 73°14'N; it was significantly further north than he had been the year before. *Swan* of Hull lay even further to the north but *Dee* of Aberdeen was close by and the Dundee ships *Thomas* and *Advice* about six miles away. Harrison of *Norfolk* and Thomas Taylor of *Grenville Bay* were related through marriage and had agreed, together with other whaler captains, to remain in company rather than attempt to strike out on their own. It proved to be a life saving decision for the men of *Thomas* which was wrecked on 13 December. Conditions on the surviving ships were deteriorating rapidly by this time and several ships had survived some dangerous moments with the Arctic pack ice. Robert Wilson and Thomas

Twatt of *Grenville Bay* recorded one of many close encounters:

> '*November 4 1836*
> *All this day the ice has been turning up in a dreadful manner ahead of us. At 1p.m. the* Norfolk *called all hands to saw and a watch of our men went to assist them...until we observed the floe coming close to our own ship...the ice had come to her in a very rapid manner turning up as high as our hawse holes...making the vessel tremble which caused all hands to have [their] cloths in readiness. God alone knows what would have become of us had our ship gone at this time*'.[26]

Some of the men exhibited the first symptoms of scurvy during December and many others were frostbitten after their exertions in saving the crew of *Thomas.*

> '*We heard today that there was a man dead in the* Advice *with scurvy*', wrote Robert Wilson on *Grenville Bay* '...*This is the first case of that kind but we have every reason to believe that it will not be the last.*' [27]

Wilson's prophecy reflected the deepening depression felt by many of the men. Thomas Crowther on *Norfolk* wrote on 15 January 1837:

> '...*The frost is very severe and the ice has been pressing to a great height all around us. I must say that everything is mixed with mercy. To look around us anyone would think it impossible for a ship to drift down this strait in safety in such a body of heavy ice. If anything were to happen to our ship now the Lord knows what would become of us, for a man could not survive many hours upon the ice owing to the severity of the weather.*'[28]

The death toll was already increasing as Crowther wrote and his own shipmates were soon to succumb to the disease. On 3 February 1837, Stephen Gamblin, master of *Dee* died during the night. He was the fifth fatality on the Aberdeen ship and his death was bitterly felt by Captain Taylor of *Grenville Bay.* Gamblin was a North Shields man and he and Taylor were old friends. Taylor arranged for the preservation of Gamblin's body which was placed in a coffin in the stern boat.[29] By 15 February *Norfolk* and her companions drew close to the Arctic Circle. On 1 March the open sea was in view but it took another two weeks for the ships to clear the ice. There had been nine deaths on *Norfolk* by this time and three on *Grenville Bay*, but few of the surviving seamen were fit to go aloft and many of them died during a stormy Atlantic passage.

Given the problems associated with the voyage of *Cove* in 1836, the Admiralty had refused several petitions from the whaler owners to equip another relief ship.[30] As an alternative many of the whalers sailing out to the Arctic grounds in the spring of 1837 carried extra provisions purchased from the proceeds of a benevolent fund. The Newcastle ships *Lord Gambier* and *Lady Jane* sailed from the Tyne in March 1837 with food, fuel and clothing provided by a relief committee of shipowners and merchants. The first of the trapped whalers to benefit from these supplies was *Norfolk* of Berwick, which met *Lord Gambier* on 30 March. Richard Warham, master of *Lord Gambier* described the meeting.

'*Ship:* Lord Gambier, *March 31 1837*
Mouth of the Davis Straits
Lat. *58°30' N*
Long. *51°30' W*

Sir,

At sunset last night a strange sail hove in sight to which we bore down with a fresh breeze from the northward and in a short time I had the pleasure of going on board the Norfolk. *Many of the people are sick and out of sixty hands, including a number of the crew of the* Thomas, *sixteen have died...*

...The mortality has chiefly been confined to the present month so that I sincerely hope that our falling in with the ship...may have the effect of checking disease and preserving the lives of the unfortunate men...' [31]

There were two further deaths on *Norfolk* before she reached Stromness. The supplies received from *Lord Gambier* and later from *Joseph Green* and *Superior* of Peterhead had been crucial to the health of the crew. The other ships were nothing like as fortunate.

On the same day that Warham wrote his letter, *Grenville Bay* was battered by severe gales a hundred miles to the south of him:

'*...None could go aloft...*', wrote the seamen on board *Grenville Bay*, '*...all our sails are hanging loose and exposed to the gale...we are now in a melancholy state and but a dark outlook, our strength is fast decaying and our sails going to rags*'.[32]

Sixteen men had already died on *Grenville Bay* before she received assistance from other ships on 19 April. Within a few hours *Grenville Bay* was surrounded by seven ships whose captains agreed to provide one man each to navigate the whaler back to Orkney.

> '*This was so much comfort to us as we are unable to express*', wrote Robert Wilson, '*...those men who came on board of us were very kind and rendered every assistance that was within their power...*[they] *sent up our topgallant yards and made all sail on the ship that could be allowed.*'[33]

Grenville Bay received further supplies from other ships, including *Lady Jane*, outward bound to the whaling grounds, and eventually reached Stromness on 27 April. *Norfolk* arrived the same day. The combined death toll of both ships was 36 men.

Norfolk arrived off Berwick on 4 May and anchored in the bay to await the tide. News of her arrival spread rapidly around the town and Berwick came to a standstill. The ramparts of the old town walls were soon crowded with spectators anxious for news of their menfolk. It was an historic event in the history of Berwick. At high water *Norfolk* weighed, entered the Tweed and slowly approached her moorings at the Carr Rock:

> '*...on landing at the pier Captain Harrison and two of the crew were met by the mayor and some of the owners, by whom, and by troops of friends as* [they] *passed along were cordially congratulated on their return from regions so inhospitable and perilous.*'[34]

Similar scenes welcomed the arrival of *Grenville Bay* at Shields the following day.

Despite the public welcome they received, the voyages of both ships were as financially disastrous to the owners as they had been terrible for their crews. Epic stories of hardship and adventure in the Arctic made for good journalism but bad economics. Thomas Richard Batson, the owner of *Grenville Bay*, persevered for a few more years by using his existing financial assets. But the writing was on the wall. In six voyages between 1835 and 1840 *Grenville Bay* returned to Tyneside with an average annual catch of 5.5 whales yielding 68 tuns of oil. But the successful voyage of 1838 was exceptional and without it *Grenville Bay*'s seasonal average was just 1.8 whales and 33 tuns of oil.[35] Poor catches of this order were unsustainable and hardly covered the expenses of a normal voyage. Batson's flagship *Lord Gambier* fared little better during these years and he probably lost in excess of £8,000 on the voyages of his whalers between 1835 and 1840. Moreover, Batson was also obliged to bear his share of the losses sustained by *Norfolk* and *Lady Jane*.

The Berwick ship was the first to go. She was sold to owners at Hull in 1838 and lost in general trade within a year. In December 1840, William Smith Batson, one of the remaining partners in the Tweed Bank, was declared bankrupt and the bank itself failed in 1841. The first historian of Northumberland banking concluded that:

'...*several of the partners were engaged in the whale trade and in that business lost large sums of money*...'.[36]

Thomas Richard Batson was left with debts of £36,000, an enormous sum of money for those years, and in October 1842 he compromised his debt for £12,000. In paying the settlement Batson sold all of his interests in Tyne whalers to Matthew Plummer. He had clearly been unwise to maintain such a singular financial interest in whaling ships for so long.[37]

References

1. One of the best accounts of the economic circumstances which contributed to the decline of British whaling is Jackson, G. *The British Whaling Trade*, Chapter 6, pp.117-131. See also Davis L. E., Gallman R.E. and Hutchins, T.D., 'Technology, Productivity and Profits: British-American Whaling Competition in the North Atlantic 1816-1842', *Oxford Economic Papers*, XXIX, (1987), pp.738-759. For a local perspective see Barrow, T. 'The Decline of British Whaling in Arctic Canada, 1820-1850: A Case Study of Newcastle-upon-Tyne', *The Northern Mariner/Le Marin du nord*, VIII, No.4 (October 1998), pp. 35-54.

2. Public Record Office (PRO), ZHC 1/772, Accounts relating to the Whale Fisheries, BPP, 1823.

3. Scoresby reckoned that the blubber of a Greenland whale yielded about 9½ tuns of oil, while that of a Davis Straits whale yielded fourteen tuns. Scoresby, W. *An Account of the Arctic Regions with a History and Description of the Northern Whale Fishery*, II, p.391.

4. Jackson, G. *Whaling Trade*. Appendix 9.

5. The wreck of *Esk* in 1826 was widely covered by provincial newspapers. Another account can be followed in Dykes, J. *Yorkshire's Whaling Days* (Dalesmen Books, 1980), pp.35-37.

6. Hull Central Library (HCL), ND 8189, Reel 1. Logbook of the *Eagle* of Hull. Entries for 26 and 27 June 1830.

7. Logbook of *Cove* of South Shields, George Palmer Collection. Entry for 12 October 1830.

8. PRO, BT 98/519, Crew List and Agreement of the *Camden* of Whitby 1836. A copy of the crew list can be found in the Appendix.

9. Barrow, A. 'North East Coast Whale Fishery, 1750-1850', University of Northumbria, Ph.D (1989), Table 40.2, p.173.

10. Between 1825 and 1834, European whalers (principally British) returned a total landed catch of 8,510 whales. See Mitchell, E and Reeves, R. *Catch History and Cumulative Catch Estimates of Initial Population Size of Ceteceans in the Eastern Canadian Arctic.* Report of the International Whaling Commission, XXXI (1981), p.650.

11. Jackson, G. *Whaling Trade*, Appendix 9.

12. James Williamson was born in Lancashire in 1814 and sailed as the surgeon of *Lady Jane* before setting up in practice as a doctor at South Shields. After his retirement he moved to London, where he died in 1899. The journal of his voyage in *Lady Jane,* now in the possession of a descendant Mr. M. Williamson of Kings Lynn, Norfolk, provides a graphic description of the whaler's ice-drift voyage. The author is grateful to Mr. Williamson for allowing access to the journal. A photocopy is also in the possession of the Town Docks Museum, Hull.

13. Williamson Journal, 5 October 1835.

14. Taylor's letter, published in the *Newcastle Journal*, 9 January 1836 was sent by *Harmony* of Hull which broke clear of the ice before *Grenville Bay*.

15. *Newcastle Journal*, 9 January 1836.

16. The cook of *Grenville Bay* was lost overboard during the Atlantic passage.

17. Williamson Journal, 17 December 1835.

18. George Francis wrote the letter, dated 18 May 1836, to a relative after the arrival of *Lady Jane* at North Shields. Williamson included a copy of the letter in his journal.

19. *Newcastle Chronicle*, 2 April 1836.

20. *Newcastle Chronicle*, 23 April 1836.

21. *Newcastle Chronicle*, 16 April 1836.

22. *Newcastle Chronicle*, 23 April 1836.

23. *Newcastle Chronicle*, 23 April 1836.

24. The Trustees of the Greenland Fund subsequently identified over one hundred dependant relatives of local seamen from *Grenville Bay* and *Lady Jane*. They also remitted funds for the welfare of dependants of the Orkneymen who lost their lives in *Lady Jane* in 1835-36.

25. *Newcastle Journal*, 12 March 1836.

26. Journal of Robert Wilson and Thomas Twatt, seamen on board *Grenville Bay* of Newcastle, quoted in Troup, J. *The Icebound Whalers* (Stromness, 1987).

27. Journal of Wilson and Twatt. Entry for 26 December 1836.

28. The original manuscript of Crowther's journal remains in private hands and has not been seen by the author. The surviving fragment of the journal was first used in a public lecture at Spittal, near Berwick in 1920. It was reprinted in full in the *Spittal News*, February 1968. The accuracy of the positions given by Crowther and the corroborative evidence of the journals written by David Gibb on *Dee* and Robert Wilson and Thomas Twatt on *Grenville Bay* leaves little doubt that it is genuine.

29. There were six other seamen from north-east England in the crew of *Dee*, all of them died of scurvy. Amongst them were the spectioneer, George Dawson from Sunderland, and the cook, Samuel Brown from North Shields. Both of them were Greenland veterans; Dawson was 56 and Brown 67 at the time of their death.

30. The editor of the *Newcastle Journal* made several bitter attacks on the Admiralty for its failure to send a relief ship. See, for example, *Newcastle Journal*, 6 May 1837.

31. *Newcastle Journal*, 6 May 1837.

32. Journal of Wilson and Twatt. Entry for 31 March 1837.

33. Journal of Wilson and Twatt. Entries for 19 and 20 April 1837.

34. *Newcastle Journal*, 13 May 1837.

35. Barrow. A. 'Whale Fishery', Ph.D (1989), p.178.

36. Phillips, M. *A History of Banks, Bankers and Banking in Northumberland, Durham and North Yorkshire* (1894), p.162.

37. T.R. Batson's financial demise can be followed in Barrow, T. 'The Decline of British Whaling', *The Northern Mariner/Le Marin du Nord*, VIII, 1998, pp.35-54.

8

'...So far as this port is concerned the whale fishing trade will be extinct...'

[*Newcastle Courant*, 6 October 1849]

The End of an Era

The Rediscovery of Cumberland Sound 1840-41

Events in Arctic Canada in 1835-36 and 1836-37 marked a real turning point in the decline of the Davis Straits Fishery and stimulated a thorough re-examination of the structure and methods of British whaling enterprise. The idea of establishing a permanent settlement of whalermen on Baffin Island or some other suitable place soon became a subject of vigorous debate in nautical literature. Sir James Clark Ross R. N., who had taken command of the ex-Tyne whaler *Cove* in an attempt to relieve the trapped vessels in 1836, was an enthusiastic supporter of the project. Ross favoured the development of a whaling station: '*...on the deeply indented northern shore of Cumberland Straits, or in about Latitude 64°N.*'[1] The problem associated with acting upon Ross's suggestion was that the location of Cumberland Sound was not certainly known. Remarkably, it had not been visited by British navigators since it was first discovered by John Davis at the end of the sixteenth century. British whalers usually took their departure from Cape Dyer or Cape Walsingham which lay to the north of Cumberland Sound. As a consequence this part of Baffin Island remained largely unexplored. William Penny, master of the Aberdeen whaler *Neptune*, began the process of rediscovery in 1839. In that year Penny returned to Aberdeen with Eenoolooapik, a young Innuit who had provided several whaler captains with an accurate account of what they took to be Cumberland Sound. Amongst them were two of the Newcastle captains, Richard Warham of *Lord Gambier* and George Harrison of *Lady Jane*. Both were experienced whalermen and together with William Penny made a significant contribution to the rediscovery and charting of this region of Arctic Canada.

Richard Warham (1796-1853) was the son of a Leeds ironmonger who settled in Newcastle during the Napoleonic War. Warham shipped aboard a local whaler at South Shields in 1812 and assumed command of *British Queen* in 1820 during a period of renewed interest in Arctic exploration. The discovery of the Baffin Bay Fishery by British whalers in 1817 revived an official interest in the existence of a North-West Passage, from the Atlantic to the Pacific Oceans. In 1818 Parliament offered a substantial reward for its discovery, and the first of a series of expeditions under Captain Edward Parry sailed the following year. At least three of the Newcastle ships visited Baffin Bay in 1820, including Warham on his maiden voyage as master of *British Queen*. During the course of the voyage Warham made one of the earliest recorded contacts with the Innuit of Baffin Island and he continued to express an interest in the progress of discovery ships over the following years.[2]

With the exception of some of the Whitby captains like Banks or Scoresby, George Harrison (1796-1870) was probably the best known of all the whaler captains of north-east England. Born at Hartley in Northumberland, Harrison first went to sea on a local collier in 1809. He survived the press-gang and shipwreck off the Lincolnshire coast before shipping aboard a whaler at Hull in 1819. Harrison took command of *Norfolk* at Berwick in 1827 and twice survived the experience of besetment during the winters of 1835-36 and 1836-37. When *Norfolk* was withdrawn from the whaling trade, Harrison transferred his skills to Tyneside and assumed command of *Lady Jane* in 1838. Given his earlier experiences, Harrison could claim to have had a vested interest in the rediscovery of Cumberland Sound. When he returned from the Arctic in 1839 the Newcastle papers reported that:

> '*The captain of the* Lady Jane *of this port has, we understand, an astonishingly neat and so far as the captain can tell an accurate chart of the sea and land...drawn by the intelligent native which Captain Penny has brought over. From the information which the captain of the* Lady Jane *obtained from the Eskimo as to the regions where the whales now go to breed, he hopes to avail himself to some profitable extent, should he be spared to visit the Fishery another year and the weather and state of the ice allow him access to the quarter pointed out to him by the young man brought by the captain of the* Neptune.'[3]

Harrison clearly intended to return to that region of Baffin Island in 1840 and subsequent newspaper reports confirm that he did so, in company with Richard Warham of *Lord Gambier.*

> '*After encountering some of the usual difficulties and delays of ice sailing,* Lord Gambier *in company with* Lady Jane *and some other vessels, succeeded in forcing their way through a rather compact body of ice into an inlet (which Captain Warham has named Northumberland Inlet)*'.[4]

Newcastle Whaling Fleet in the Arctic, c.1835. *J.W. Carmichael.*

The vessel in the foreground is **Lord Gambier**, with **Grenville Bay** to the right and **Lady Jane** in the background. The crew of the whaleboat in the foreground have raised a flag to show that they are 'fast' to a whale and their signal has been acknowledged from **Lord Gambier**.
The Kendall Whaling Museum, Sharon, Massachusetts, USA.

Mouth of the Tyne, 1847 *J.W. Carmichael.*

The artist shows the arrival of the Tyne's veteran whaler **Lady Jane**, with her whaleboats at their davits and a mayday garland on the main topgallant stay. **Lady Jane** was wrecked in Melville Bay in June 1849.

Port of Tyne Authority.

1789

Copy of a Licence of a Whale Boat No. 1 belonging the Ship Loyalty Robt. Jackson Master

No. 1342

By the Commissioners for Executing the Office of Lord High Admiral of Great Britain and Ireland &c

Suffer the Whale Boat No. 1 clench built Length Twenty seven 6/12 feet Breadth Five 9/12 feet — Depth Two feet three Inches — Plank half an Inch thick Timber one Inch Square rowing with six Oars, and belonging to the Ship Loyalty of Stockton whereof Robert Jackson is Master, intended to be employed in the Greenland Trade to pass without any Lett, Hindrance, Seizure, or Molestation; — provided it shall appear, by Certificate on the Back hereof from the Collector, Compr. or other proper Officer of the Customs, that the Master, or the owner hath given Security to the Satisfaction, by Bond to His Majesty, His Heirs and Successors, in double the value of the said Boat, with Condition that she shall not be employed in Smuggling or any other illicit Trade. Given under our Hands, and the Seal of the Office of Admiralty the Twenty fourth day of February in the Year of our Lord 1789

signed { R: Hopkins
Bayham
Hood

Whaleboat licence for the **Loyalty** of Stockton, 1789. Whether whaleboat No.1 was ever.... *"employed in smuggling or any other illicit trade"*, is not recorded.

Public Record Office.

To be SOLD, by AUCTION,

AT Robert Coats's, the Green Dragon, in Stockton upon Tees, on Wednesday the First of January, 1794, at Two o'Clock in the Afternoon,

The BRIGANTINE LOYALTY, of Stockton, Robert Jackson, Master, lying at Portrack, near Stockton.—She is a Square-sterned Vessel, of about 216 Tons Burthen, Register Admeasurement, shifts without Ballast, carries about 16 Keels of Coals, is remarkably well found, has a complete Set of Boats, Casks, Whale Lines, Utensils, and Instruments for the Greenland or Davis's Streights Fishery, is allowed to be a nimble, active Ship, in that Trade, is doubled several Strokes from her Binds downward, has been lately new docked and repaired in her Upperworks, is also fit for the Coal or Baltic Trade; and may be sent to Sea without any Expence, except Victualing for the Voyage.

A Purchaser wishing to continue the Vessel in the Fishery, may have a convenient Boiling-House, with good Warehouses for the Oil Stores, &c. at Portrack, at a lower Rent than in most of the Ports in the North of England; and few Places are so well, and none better situated than Stockton, for victualling and manning a Ship in that Trade.

An Inventory of the Materials, Fishing Stores, &c. may be seen on Application to the Master, at Hartlepool; or to Robert Lumley, in Stockton.

William Scoresby Snr. (1760-1829). One of several Whitby whaler captains from Pickering in North Yorkshire, Scoresby became a legend in his own lifetime.

Hull Maritime Museum.

William Scoresby Jnr. (1789-1857). Whaler captain, navigator and Arctic scientist. Scoresby's **An Account of the Arctic Regions**, 1820, remains a basic work of reference.

Hull Maritime Museum.

George Palmer (1784-1866), master of **Cove** and father of the better known Charles Mark Palmer who began building iron steam ships at Jarrow in 1852.

Courtesy of Stephen Wolfenden.

George Harrison (1796-1870). Master of the **Norfolk** of Berwick and **Lady Jane** of Newcastle. Few whalermen with Harrison's experience ended their seafaring careers with a full complement of fingers and toes!

Whalebone arch at the Stanners, Morpeth, Northumberland. The arch is one of several surviving examples scattered throughout North East England.

Courtesy of Nick Redman

The arch at **Sleights** near Whitby seen in 1979, when it was at least 180 years old. The wooden goose was a 1964 replacement for the original eagle figurehead from a sailing ship that was blown down in a gale in 1919 and not replaced. The bones were removed about 1990.

Whalebone arch which stood at the entrance to a builders yard in Gallowgate, Newcastle. St. Andrew's church can be seen to the left.

Newcastle Libraries and Information Service.

Courtesy of John Gaskin

The **Valliant** arch as it appeared after it was re-erected at the Ryedale Folk Museum, Hutton-le-Hole. It had originally formed the entrance gate to Westfield Lodge but was demolished by a tank in 1944! The inscription **Valliant**, Whitby 1792, probably refers to the first of three whalers of that name.

Peterhead Whaling Crew, c.1860.

A unique photograph of the crew of a Peterhead whaler assembled in the oil yard at Keith Inch.

Aberdeenshire Heritage.

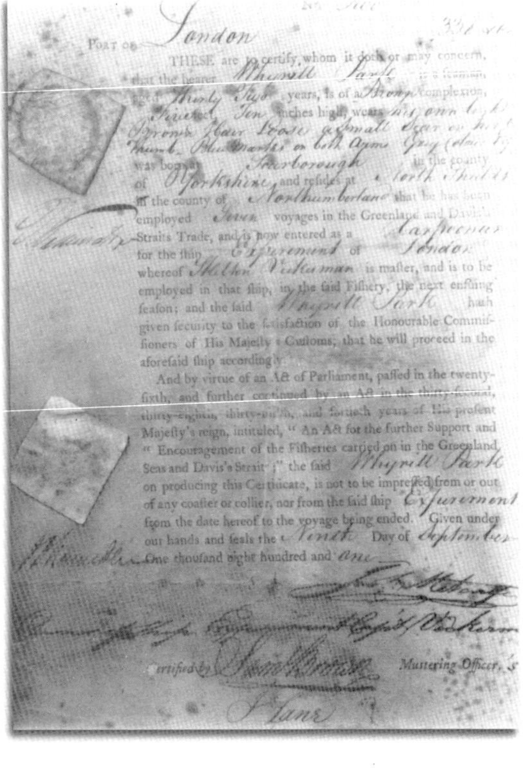

PORT OF London

THESE are to certify, whom it doth or may concern, that the bearer Whyrell Park is a feaman, aged Thirty Two years, is of a Brown complexion, Five feet Ten inches high, wears his own [illegible] Brown Hair Loose a Small Scar on his [illegible] thumb Blue marks on both Arms Grey [illegible] was born at Scarborough in the county of Yorkshire, and refides at North Shields in the county of Northumberland that he has been employed Seven voyages in the Greenland and Davis's Straits Trade, and is now entered as a Carpenter for the fhip Experiment of London whereof [illegible] Vickerman is mafter, and is to be employed in that fhip, in the faid Fifhery, the next enfuing feafon; and the faid Whyrell Park hath given fecurity to the fatisfaction of the Honourable Commiffioners of His Majefty's Cuftoms, that he will proceed in the aforefaid fhip accordingly.

And by virtue of an Act of Parliament, paffed in the twenty-fixth, and further continued by an Act in the thirty-fecond, thirty-eighth, thirty-ninth, and fortieth years of His prefent Majefty's reign, intituled, "An Act for the further Support and "Encouragement of the Fifheries carried on in the Greenland Seas and Davis's Strait;" the faid Whyrell Park on producing this Certificate, is not to be impreffed from or out of any coafter or collier, nor from the faid fhip Experiment from the date hereof to the voyage being ended. Given under our hands and feals the Ninth Day of September One thoufand eight hundred and one

Certified by [illegible] Muftering Officer.

Impress exemption certificate of a Greenland seaman, 1801

Pheonix and Camden entering Whitby harbour, c. 1834 *George Chambers.*

Both vessels were owned by the Chapman family and sailed together between 1833 and 1836.

The Kendall Whaling Museum, Sharon, Massachusetts, USA.

Cove in the Arctic, c. 1830 *George Palmer Collection.*

Cove, Cpt. George Palmer, was probably the first whaler from North East England to sail to the Baffin Bay Fishery after its discovery in 1817.

Courtesy of Stephen Wolfenden.

Subsequently, much of the credit for the 'discovery' was claimed by William Penny (1809-1892), who was then at the threshold of a famous career.[5] Penny's initiatives with the Innuit of Durban Island undoubtedly paved the way for the Cumberland Sound discoveries. Nevertheless when he returned to Aberdeen with Eenoolooapik in 1839, he clearly did so with the full knowledge and approval of the Newcastle captains. Subsequently, when Penny arrived off the entrance to Cumberland Sound in the following year, he found that *Lord Gambier* and *Lady Jane* were already there. The voyage of the Newcastle men was marred only by poor whaling and the death of William Jameson, surgeon of *Lady Jane*, who was killed in a shooting accident. Jameson was buried on the north shore of Cumberland Sound on 12 August 1840: '*...near the spot is a lofty peaked mountain which was named in memory of him, Jameson's Monument.*'[6]

Warham and Harrison returned to Cumberland Sound again in 1841. Warham's familiarity with its long indented coastline and the Innuit who inhabited the region is apparent from his journal of the voyage. His chart of Cumberland Sound, which he called Northumberland Inlet, and part of the journal of *Lord Gambier* were subsequently published in the *Journal of the Royal Geographical Society* in 1842.

Lord Gambier in company with *Lady Jane* arrived off the entrance to Cumberland Sound during the middle of August 1841:

> '*13 August 1841*
> *perceived the ice to the north westward much closer and very heavy...hauled to the east in the hope of getting around it and finding a passage into Northumberland Inlet...*'[7]

Running to the north-west along the northern shore of Cumberland Sound, the whalermen eventually found a secure and well populated anchorage where they remained for almost three weeks:

> '*24 August 1841*
> *the novelty of our appearance and consequent excitement having in some measure subsided amongst the Esquimaux, I took the opportunity of obtaining the attention of an elderly man...to obtain some information relative to the route of the whales. He said that the name of our present position was Annanetoote...*'

Using their whaleboats, the Greenlanders dispatched regular expeditions along the coastline, some of them sailing up to twenty miles from the ships. On 1 September, one of the boats sighted a whale but it was swimming rapidly to the south and there was little chance of catching it. By now it was late in the season and the Innuit community were pitching camp and moving south for the winter. Warham's journal recorded the steady accumulation of bay ice:

> '*4 September 1841*
> *the southernmost passage from the harbour is filled with grounded ice and no prospect of its opening until next spring...some white whales seen in the harbour...[and]...some swans observed steering their course to the southward...*'

Fearing the prospect of besetment, *Lord Gambier* weighed anchor and proceeded from the harbour on 10 September, setting a course to the south-south-east. It was an anxious time. Their egress from Cumberland Sound was not without its dangers and proved to be more difficult than their arrival just over a month before:

> '*12 September 1841*
> *Fresh breeze increased to a strong gale that forced us to close reef...wared backwards and forwards during the dark watches not without apprehensions of a lee shore...frequent snow showers prevented us from seeing the land until daybreak...*'

> '*14 September 1841*
> *Snow dispersed and we found some room among open ice to run along the land...when the breeze subsided sent the boats ahead to tow...some high-finned cachalot but no mysticete seen...*'

Lord Gambier eventually cleared the entrance to Cumberland Sound on 15 September and arrived off the Tyne on 21 October. *Lady Jane* arrived the following day. Despite their enterprise in Cumberland Sound, the commercial value of the voyages was poor. *Lord Gambier* secured a single whale and seven bottlenose whales boiling to 25 tuns of oil; *Lady Jane* was 'clean'. *Lord Gambier*'s unsuccessful voyage was the final straw for her owner, Thomas Richard Batson, who was declared a bankrupt. He was forced to sell his remaining assets to meet the demands of his creditors. It was also Warham's last voyage to the Canadian Arctic, and his surveys of Cumberland Sound were a fitting tribute to a long and successful whaling career. The journal of his 1841 voyage and the chart that accompanied it, finally confirmed the true location of that region of Baffin Island. The editor of the *Journal of the Royal Geographical Society* concluded:

> '*Whoever takes the trouble to collate Mr. Warham's account of Northumberland Inlet, with the account of Cumberland Straits in Davis's* Traverse Book, *published by Hackluyt in the third volume of his general collection of* Voyages and Travels (1600), *will see good grounds to believe that these two names designate the same inlet.*' [8]

Lord Gambier, under the command of Thomas Taylor, formerly master of *Grenville Bay*, sailed from the Tyne to the Davis Straits in 1843 and 1844, but only with moderate success. Before the year was out *Lord Gambier*, together with her whaling stores and specialist equipment, was offered for sale. She was purchased by Robert Collison of Hull and transferred to that port on 8 March 1845.[9]

Last years of the 'Lady' 1845-1849

Between 1845 and 1849 only one vessel was employed in the whaling trade from the river Tyne, *Lady Jane*, owned by Matthew Plummer & Co. Plummer had extensive shipping, industrial and commercial interests but no special interest in the whaling trade. By the 1840s fully equipped whalers like *Lady Jane* were discreet units of shipping, employing local expertise and selling their products into a local market. It seemed natural, therefore, despite the bankruptcy of Thomas Richard Batson, that Plummer should continue to use her in the whaling trade. Whether *Lady Jane* could have been so remuneratively employed in another trade is open to question and Plummer did not seem to concern himself much with the alternatives. He was wealthy enough to gamble and astute enough to read the signs. With whale oil selling at £50 per tun and whalebone for £200 per ton the profits of a single successful voyage remained an attractive proposition. Based on these prices *Lady Jane* earned over £7,000 for Matthew Plummer in 1845 and more than £15,000 in total between 1842 and 1847.[10] The success of *Lady Jane* was due in no small measure to the experience of the captain, George Harrison, who remained in command of the ship until 1847. At the beginning of that season the owners of *Lady Jane* presented Captain Harrison with some commemorative silverware '*…in testimony of meritorious service as master of the vessel*'. Harrison had experienced a particularly difficult voyage the year before and the presentation was a recognition of his skill and perseverance in extricating *Lady Jane* from hazardous circumstances and completing a successful voyage.[11] It undoubtedly influenced his decision to retire and Harrison may well have indicated his intention to do so at the end of the 1847 season. *Lady Jane* cleared the Tyne on 27 March but contrary winds held her off the coast for almost a week and Harrison was forced to put back to Shields. It was a bad start to a poor season and a disappointing end to a distinguished career.[12]

Harrison's successor as master of *Lady Jane* was John Patterson, who was already a veteran of the whaling trade when he took command. Patterson had sailed with Harrison as chief mate between 1838-1845 and relinquished command of *Lord Gambier* of Hull to become the captain of *Lady Jane* in 1848. That season was dominated by public interest in the progress of several expeditions sent by the Admiralty to search for Sir John Franklin. In July 1848 Patterson was one of a number of British whaler captains to part company with Sir James Ross' ships *Enterprise* and *Investigator* in Melville Bay. Ironically, the last ship to see Sir James Ross was *Lord Gambier* on 25 July. Patterson, finding it impossible to penetrate the middle ice from Melville Bay, turned *Lady Jane* to the south and eventually found a passage to the coast of Baffin Island. It was October before *Lady Jane* sailed for England with four whales and two bottlenose whales, a cargo which was eventually worth about £3,000. The 1849 season got off to an inauspicious start when the departure of many British whalers was delayed by snow storms and northerly gales. The redoubtable Captain Patterson and his crew were amongst the first to get away; *Lady Jane* cleared the Tyne on 8 March and survived a stormy passage to Stromness. In company with *Alexander* of Dundee and *Regalia* of Kirkaldy, *Lady Jane* rounded Cape Farewell on 19 April and entered the Davis Straits for the last time.[13] In June 1849 during her fiftieth voyage to the Arctic, *Lady Jane* and two other whalers were trapped and crushed by ice at the entrance to Melville Bay.

> '*For days previous the gales had been frequent and terrific and the seas tempestuous in the extreme. About 11 o'clock in the forenoon an alarm was raised of the floating ice setting in upon them. So suddenly did it bear down and with such force and immense masses…that they did not have the slightest chance of escaping it and were speedily cut to pieces. The first vessel destroyed was the* Superior *and immediately afterwards* Lady Jane *was literally cut in two, the masts at the same time falling overboard. In less than 2 hours not a vestige of the ship could be seen, so completely had the ice covered her…*'[14]

In reporting the loss of the ship the Newcastle newspapers predicted that:

> '*…so far as this port is concerned, the whale fishing trade will be extinct,*' the article continued, '*it is but due to the owners to add, that had it not been for their enterprising spirit, the vessel would not have continued so long pursuing a trade so hazardous and under such disadvantageous circumstances.*'[15]

The loss of *Lady Jane* severed a connection with Arctic enterprise that had endured on Tyneside for almost a century.

Postscript

During the 1850s two technological developments in marine engineering, iron hulls and steam propulsion, offered new opportunities to exploit the Whale Fishery. Steam propulsion in particular, gave whalermen enormous advantages over the old sailing whalers. It shortened voyage times to and from the grounds and provided a greater capacity to bore through pack-ice and escape besetment. Palmer's Shipyard at Jarrow began building iron-hulled, screw-driven steamships in 1852 and pioneered the construction of the first, purpose-built, iron-screw whaling barque, appropriately named *Innuit*, which was launched at Jarrow on 21 April 1857. *Innuit* was built for the Arctic Steam Fishing Company of Peterhead and undertook her maiden voyage to the whaling grounds in the same year. She was a remarkable vessel in many ways. Her iron hull had seven bulkheads divided into a number of smaller compartments used for the storage of blubber in bulk.[16] Palmers went on to construct several other steam whalers over the next few years, including the *Empress of India* in 1859. *Empress of India* was a huge whaler by contemporary standards, more than twice the size of most of the existing vessels then employed in the Greenland trade. She carried eleven whaleboats and a crew of 110 men. Her construction was undoubtedly influenced by a craze for huge iron steamships following the launch of Brunel's *Great Eastern* in 1857. Such was the confidence engendered by the early years of steam whaling that shipowners at Newcastle decided to enter a vessel into the Greenland Fishery for the first time since the loss of *Lady Jane*. In 1859, Laing and Stephens fitted out *Volunteer* for a voyage to the whaling grounds. She was a former Newcastle to London trader built by Palmers in 1854. *Empress of India* left the Northumberland Dock for Peterhead on 22 February and *Volunteer*, after adjusting compasses, sailed on the following day.[17] However, despite the confidence of her promoters and the pedigree of her name, *Volunteer* struck a piece of ice within a day of her arrival on the whaling grounds and sank in a few minutes. It proved to be a disastrous year for the steamers. *Empress of India* and *Innuit* were also lost in similar circumstances during the 1859 season. Iron hulls proved to be unsuitable for Arctic conditions and later designs, pioneered by Alexander Stephens & Co. at Dundee, reverted to a combination of wooden hulls and steam propulsion. Scott's *Discovery*, now preserved at Dundee, was typical of the new design, but no ships of her type sailed from the Tyne. *Volunteer* was the last Arctic whaler to sail directly from a port in north-east England.

When the focus of British whaling shifted to the southern hemisphere at the beginning of the twentieth century there was a revival of interest in the region. Irvin and Johnson of North Shields, already a famous name in trawling, established the Southern Whaling and Sealing Company in August 1911. With initial capital of £60,000 they set up a whaling station at Prince Olaf Harbour on South Georgia which eventually boasted 60 boilers and storage tanks, an engineering shop, an electrical plant and accommodation for 250-300 men.[18] The assets of the Southern Whaling and Sealing Co. were eventually transferred to Lever Brothers & Co. in September 1919, but Irvin and Johnson remained active in South Africa and the Southern Ocean throughout the inter-war years. One of their ships, *Sound of Jura*, was one of the last auxiliary sailing vessels on the Newcastle register. *Sound of Jura* was one of five peculiarly rigged barquentines built by Russell & Co. at Port Glasgow during the 1890s. She was fitted with an auxiliary diesel engine in 1911 and employed as a supply ship and whale oil carrier between Capetown and South Georgia. After the sale of the Southern Whaling and Sealing Co., *Sound of Jura* was used to supply Irvin and Johnson's newly established Kerguelan Sealing and Fishing Company. *Sound of Jura*'s registry was transferred to Capetown in 1925. She was eventually dismantled at Saldanha Bay, the base of Salvesens's South African operation in 1927.[19]

In 1929-30 two modern whale oil factory ships *Vikingen* and *Tafelberg* were completed on the Tyne; *Vikingen* by Swan Hunter and Wigham Richardson and *Tafelberg* by Armstrong Whitworth & Co. *Tafelberg*, 13,640 tons, was built for Irvin and Johnson's Kerguelan Whaling and Seal Fishing Co. at a cost of £370,000. She was then the largest and most modern whale factory ship on the British register with a capacity of 13,000 tuns of whale oil; a far cry from the 'bumper' cargo of 302 tuns brought into the Tyne by *Lady Jane* in 1832.[20] Elsewhere in the North-East other shipbuilding firms also developed an association with the whaling industry. At Middlesbrough, for example, Smiths Dock & Co. constructed 40 powerful whale catchers for Salvesen's South Shetland operation during the inter-war years.[21]

The region continued its association with whaling after the Second World War. In an atmosphere of post-war austerity, the Attlee government invested considerable time and effort promoting the nutritional value of whale meat to a sceptical British public.[22] In August 1947 small Norwegian whale catchers began to land whale meat at North Shields which was processed and marketed by Messrs. Andreas Gilberg. The animals landed at North Shields were Minke whales killed off Shetland and the British east coast as far south as the Humber. The whales were hunted between May and October as they pursued migrating shoals of herring and mackerel. In 1948 at least 40 Minke whales were killed by Norwegian whale catchers between St. Abbs Head and the mouth of the Humber, and over 100 were landed at Shields.[23] However, the resistance of the British public to the consumption of whalemeat, and the end of austerity, undermined what was always a limited market for the product and the landings ceased in the early 1950s. However, the opportunities for a prosperous resumption of commercial whaling after 1945 led Salvesen's to commission the construction of two new factory ships, *Southern Venturer* and *Southern Harvester*. Built on the Tees and maintained on the Tyne, both ships were regular visitors to the North-East during the 1950s. Some of the whalermen employed on those vessels are still active in the Shields communities 250 years after their Greenlandmen ancestors first sailed to the whaling grounds.

References

1. Ross, J.C. 'On the expediency of a settlement on the western shore of Davis Straits', *The Nautical Magazine*, Vol.VI (1837), pp.165-167.

2. 'The *British Queen* (Warham) has discovered a new colony of people, but whether those discovered by Capt. Ross or not we cannot ascertain'. *Durham County Advertiser*, 7 October 1820.

3. Port of Tyne Pilot, 20 November 1839.

4. Port of Tyne Pilot, 17 October 1840.

5. For a full account of Penny's remarkable career see Holland, C.A. 'William Penny, 1809-92, Arctic Whaler Captain', *The Polar Record*, Vol.15, No.94 (1970).

6. Port of Tyne Pilot, 17 October 1840. The site is named on Warham's chart of Northumberland Inlet.

7. This and subsequent entries from Warham's journal, together with his chart of Northumberland Inlet were published in *Journal of the Royal Geographical Society*, Volume 12 (1842), pp.21-28.

8. *Journal of the Royal Geographical Society*, Volume 12 (1842), p.21.

9. *Lord Gambier* sailed from Hull until 1853 when she was sold to owners at Kirkaldy. She was eventually wrecked in Baffin Bay in 1862.

10. Barrow, A. 'North East Coast Whale Fishery, 1750-1850', University of Northumbria, Ph.D (1989), Table 46.2 ,p.183.

11. Harrison managed to inform his owners of the difficulties he was experiencing by a letter sent on board *Diligence*, a cod fishing vessel: '...*Captain Harrison states that he never before saw so much ice in the fishery, that he had been north as far as Lat. 74°10' and south to Lat. 65°50' and could see no prospect of a passage to the westward. The flows of ice were exceedingly large and heavy. He had just got at liberty from being beset in Lat.69°40' and was proceeding to the south to make another attempt to get through the ice...*'. He eventually succeeded in doing so and *Lady Jane* caught eight whales, one fin whale and a bottlenose yielding 187 casks of blubber and six tons of whalebone. See *Newcastle Courant*, 2 October 1846.

12. Harrison was appointed Harbourmaster at Blyth in 1847 and held that office until his death in 1870. As a large shareholder in the Union Joint Stock Bank, which collapsed during the crisis of 1847, Harrison's hard-earned fortune was swallowed up in satisfying some of the claims of the creditors.

13. The progress of *Lady Jane* was reported by the surgeon of *Alexander*, John Young, whose message in a bottle was picked up in South Uist at the beginning of September 1849. See *Newcastle Chronicle*, 21 September 1849.

14. *Newcastle Chronicle*, 2 November 1849.

15. *Newcastle Courant*, 6 October 1849.

16. Keys, R.E. *A Dictionary of Tyne Sailing Ships* (1998), p.64.

17. Keys, R.E *Tyne Sailing Ships*, p.65.

18. Jackson, G. *The British Whaling Trade*, p.174.

19. Keys, R.E. *Tyne Sailing Ships*, p.649.

20. Keys, R.E. *Tyne Sailing Ships*, p.66.

21. Jackson, G. *Whaling Trade*, p.195.

22. Jackson, G. *Whaling Trade*, p.241-242.

23. Stephenson, W. 'The Lesser Rorqual in British Waters'. *Annual Report for 1949* of the Dove Marine Laboratory, Cullercoats. Marine Laboratory Committee of Kings College, Third Series, No.12 (1951).

Appendix I

Maps

1. The Whaling Grounds of the Arctic Whale Fishery
2. Drift voyages of the North-East whalers 1835-36 and 1836-37
3. Richard Warham's chart of Northumberland Inlet (Cumberland Sound) 1841

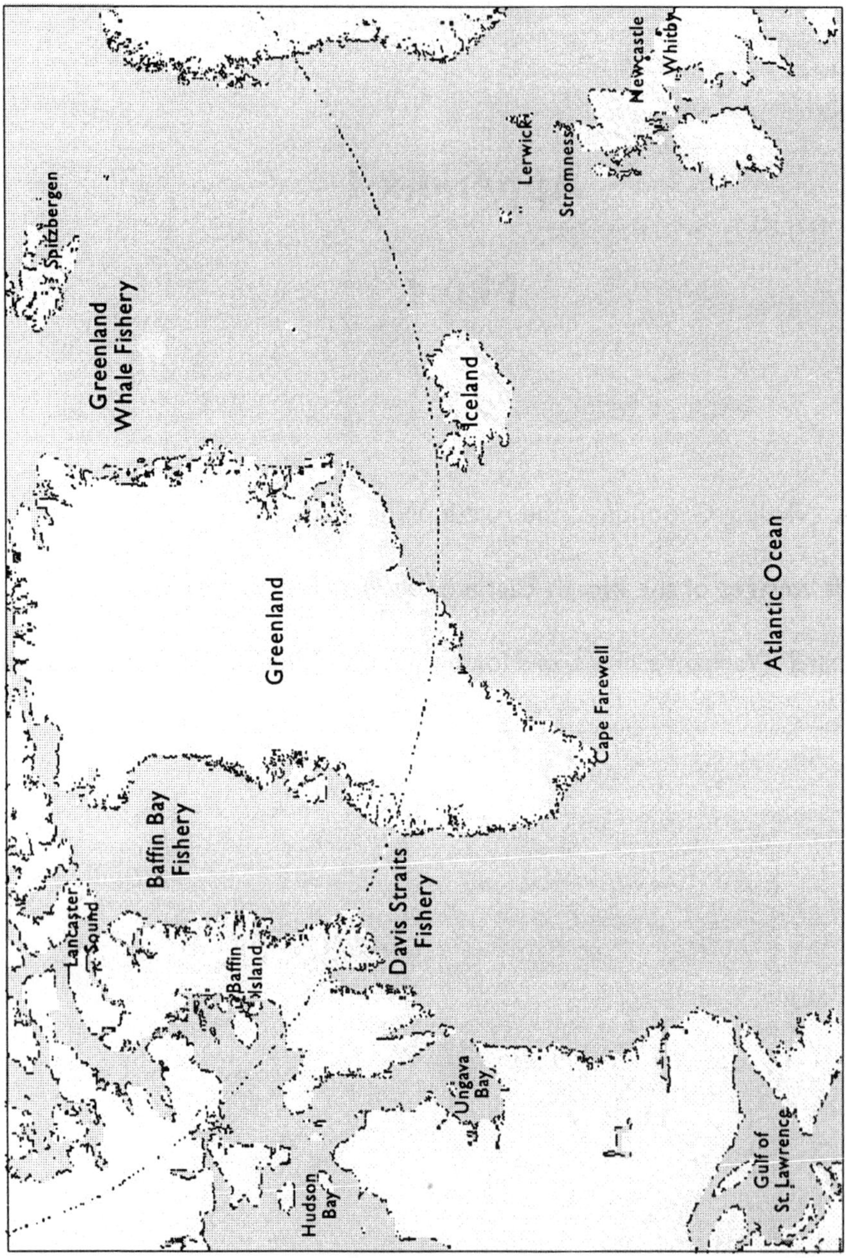

Map 1. The Whaling Grounds of the Arctic Whale Fishery

See pages 100-101

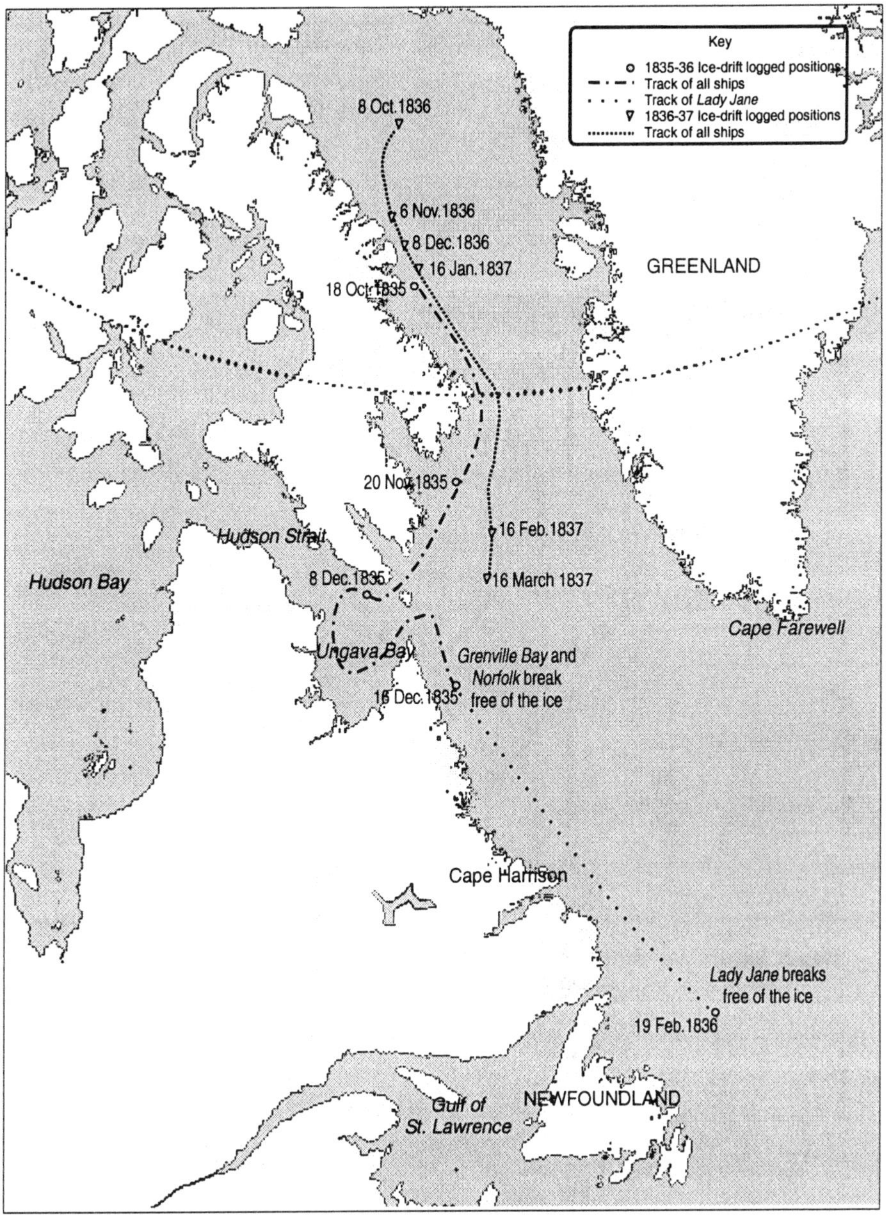

Map 2. Drift voyages of the North East whalers 1835-36 and 1836-37

See pages 111-112

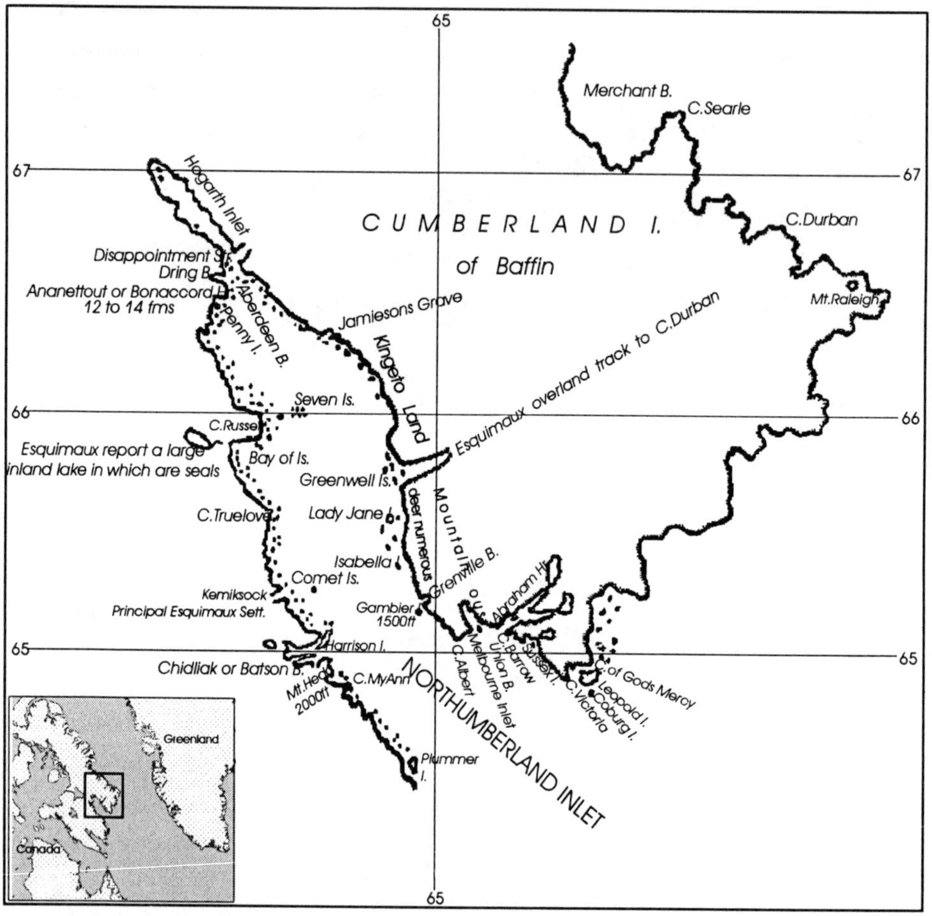

Map 3. Richard Warham's chart of Northumberland Inlet (Cumberland Sound) 1841

Appendix 2

Muster Rolls and Crew Lists of Selected North East Whalers 1753-1848

Note on Sources:
With the single exception of the crew list of *Norfolk* of Berwick for 1836-37, the surviving muster rolls and crew lists of North East whalers relate only to ships that sailed from Whitby and Shields. Of these, the Whitby muster rolls are the most comprehensive. They are available to researchers for the entire period of whaling between 1753 and 1835 and held in the collections of Whitby Literary and Philosophical Society. Whitby muster rolls can also be accessed for the period 1794-1810 within BT 98/135 and 136 at the Public Record Office. The muster rolls for 84 voyages of nineteen Tyne whalers undertaken between 1767 and 1791 are also held at the Public Record Office under references BT 98/122-134. The majority of the muster rolls for ships at both ports provide minimal information amounting to little more than a list of names. The selection presented here is drawn from the muster rolls that provide fuller details about the crews.

The introduction of Crew Lists and Agreements after the Merchant Shipping Act of 1835 came in time to capture the names of men who undertook the last whaling voyages from Whitby and Berwick in 1836. Crew lists also survive for fourteen voyages of the Tyne whalers between 1836-1848, some of which are reproduced here.

Sea Nymph, 1753

Port: Whitby

Name	*Position*	*Where Born/Abode*
James Wilson	Master	Sunderland
Anthony Aires	Mate	Shields
John Dennison	Second mate	Shields
Henry Rickaby	Surgeon	Durham
Anthony Younger	Bosun/Harpooner	London
George Hymers	Spectioneer	Shields
William Harring	Harpooner	London
John Weatherley	Harpooner	London
Thomas Stafford	Harpooner	Sunderland
Thomas Grey	Harpooner	Whitby
Peter Benson	Harpooner	London
William Cook	Boatsteerer	Shields
Robert Waugh	Boatsteerer	Sunderland
Nathan Wilkins	Boatsteerer	Yarmouth
John Johnson	Boatsteerer	Guisborough
John Asplin	Boatsteerer	London
John Chambers	Boatsteerer	Carlton
William Doram	Boatsteerer	London
Francis Banks	Line manager	Stockton
James Stewart	Line manager	Sunderland
John Anderson	Line manager	Stockton
Thomas Younger	Line manager	Sunderland
Ralph Peel	Line manager	Sunderland
William Walmsley	Line manager	Liverpool
Robert Whitfield	Line manager	London
Henry Banks	Seaman	-
William Jeffels	Cooper	Whitby
Abel Palmer	Seaman	Robin Hood's Bay
William Fawcett	Seaman	Stokesley
William Thompson	Seaman	Whitby
John Bickford	Seaman	Portsmouth
William Aldridge	Seaman	Thorn
William Prudham	Cook	Robin Hood's Bay
John Carrol	Cook's mate	Egton

(continued)

***Sea Nymph*, 1753**

Port: Whitby

Name	*Position*	*Where Born/Abode*
William Bain	Seaman	Guisborough
William Lazenby	Seaman	Stockton
Thomas Ash	Seaman	Poole
Richard Ramshaw	Seaman	Weymouth
Isaac Harrison	Seaman	Whitby
Robert Pratt	Seaman	Bridlington
John Brown	Seaman	Scarborough
William Campion	Seaman	Pickering
Thomas Harbottle	Seaman	Sunderland
John Morris	Seaman	Newcastle
Edward Cook	Carpenter	Whitby
William Cuthbert	Carpenter's mate	Whitby
Philip Parker	Seaman	Ipswich
Soloman Hitchin	Seaman	Whitby
John Harkin	Seaman	Thorn

Source: WLPS, No. 93

Henry and Mary, 1756

Port: Whitby

Name	*Position*	*Where Born/Abode*
Thomas Todd	Master	Whitby
George Ogilvy	Surgeon	Edinburgh
Christopher Greenman	Mate	Whitby
Manken Prudom	Harpooner	Whitby
William Aspell	Harpooner	Newcastle
Juneus Webster	Harpooner	Whitby
Nicholas Hodgson	Harpooner	Whitby
Jonathan Brown	Harpooner	Whitby
Thomas Harens	Harpooner	Whitby
Jonathan Nicholson	Boatsteerer	Whitby
Jonathan Ventress	Boatsteerer	Whitby
George Collins	Boatsteerer	Whitby
Ingram Estill	Boatsteerer	Whitby
William Andrew	Boatsteerer	Whitby
Jonathan Ripley	Boatsteerer	Whitby
Andrew Reynolds	Line manager	Whitby
Jonathan Boon	Line manager	Whitby
Robert Lumley	Line manager	Whitby
Edward Arnold	Line manager	Whitby
Jonathan Garbutt	Cooper	Whitby
Richard Storey	Cooper's mate	Whitby
Matthew Marshall	Carpenter	Whitby
Thomas Bound	Carpenter's mate	Whitby
Richard Appleton	Cook	Whitby
Ralph Matthewson	Cook's mate	Whitby

+ 17 seaman

Source: WLPS, No. 43

Volunteer, 1772

Port: Whitby

Name	*Position*	*Where Born/Abode*
William Coulson	Master	Whitby
Mathew Smith	Mate	Whitby
Jeremiah Boyes	Second mate	Whitby
William Kidd	Surgeon	Whitby
John Brown	Spectioneer	Whitby
Jacob Grimes	Harpooner	Whitby
Richard Grice	Harpooner	Whitby
Thomas Robson	Harpooner	Whitby
William Coates	Carpenter	Whitby
Jonathan Ferndill	Second carpenter	Whitby
Thomas Webster	Boatsteerer	Whitby
Thomas Wilson	Boatsteerer	Robin Hood's Bay
William Collins	Boatsteerer	Robin Hood's Bay
Joseph Paxton	Boatsteerer	Whitby
James Glad	Boatsteerer	Whitby
Bethel Right	Boatsteerer	Scarborough
Joseph Fidler	Line manager	Sleights
John Curbes	Line manager	Sunderland
Thomas Morley	Line manager	Whitby
John Scott	Line manager	Whitby
George Richardson	Line manager	Whitby
John Asbit	Line manager	Whitby
William Raw	Cooper	Whitby
Samuel Gambles	Cook	Whitby
William Rowantree	Second cook	Whitby
Thomas Ogle	Seaman	Whitby
Armstrong Watson	Seaman	Whitby
Daniel Gunn	Seaman	Whitby
Robert Dale	Seaman	Dundee
Robert Elliott	Seaman	Whitby
Thomas Potts	Seaman	Whitby
Hugh Dryden	Seaman	Whitby
Alexander Steward	Seaman	Whitby
Francis Bovil	Seaman	Whitby
Robert Cooper	Seaman	Whitby
William Chapman	Servant	Whitby
William Barry	Servant	Whitby
Robert Craggs	Servant	Whitby
Henry Stephenson	Servant	Whitby
Edmond Taylor	Servant	Whitby

Source: WLPS, Book 10 p. 48.

Providence, 1775

Port: Whitby

Name	*Position*	*Where Born/Abode*
Thomas Carlile	Master	Whitby
George Halleyman	Mate	Whitby
William Taylor	Second mate	Whitby
Samuel Starling	Carpenter	Whitby
William Esdell	Carpenter's mate	Whitby
William Lawson	Cook	Whitby
William Jarret	Doctor	Hull
Thomas Sherwood	Cooper	Whitby
William Ward	Harpooner	Whitby
George Jones	Harpooner	Whitby
Jonathan Taylor	Harpooner	Whitby
Michael Jameson	Harpooner	Whitby
Benjamin Cook	Boatsteerer	Whitby
Richard Todd	Boatsteerer	Whitby
William Audos	Boatsteerer	Whitby
William Jones	Boatsteerer	Whitby
Charles Edwardson	Boatsteerer	Whitby
James Pallas	Line manager	Sunderland
James Crow	Line manager	Whitby
Thomas Robson	Line manager	Whitby
William Smith	Line manager	Whitby
Ralph Childs	Line manager	Sunderland
John Scott	Seaman	Whitby
Robert Richardson	Seaman	Whitby
Jacob Francis	Seaman	Whitby
Owen Finger	Seaman	Sunderland
William Anderson	Seaman	Whitby
Samuel Taylor	Seaman	Whitby
William Garbutt	Seaman	Whitby
Thomas Metcalf	Seaman	Whitby
Isaac Fotherley	Seaman	Whitby
William Carling	Seaman	Whitby

Source: WLPS, No. 80

Friendship, 1776

Port: Whitby

Name	*Position*	*Where Born/Abode*
George Ismay	Master	Newcastle
Nicholas Hodgson	Mate	Whitby
Miles Ismay	Harpooner	Newcastle
John Mote	Harpooner	Newcastle
John Wray	Harpooner	Newcastle
James Pottinger	Harpooner	Shields
Henry Ditchburn	Harpooner	Shields
Edward Cutter	Harpooner	Shields
Thomas Pattison	Boatsteerer	Shields
William Wrightson	Boatsteerer	Shields
Caleb Atkinson	Boatsteerer	Shields
John Mitchell	Boatsteerer	Shields
Richard Joicey	Boatsteerer	Newcastle
Peter Ford	Boatsteerer	Newcastle
Alex Bookless	Boatsteerer	Newcastle
George Hutchinson	Line manager	
James Fairweather	Line manager	
George Knight	Line manager	
James Robson	Line manager	
Charles Port	Line manager	
Rowland Tweddle	Line manager	
John Mills	Line manager	

Source: WLPS, No. 84

Kitty, 1783

Port: Shields

Name	*Age*	*Position*	*Where Born/Abode*
John Lattimore	45	Master	Newcastle
George Starkie	35	Mate	Shields
Henry Davidson	22	Surgeon	Shields
Dobinson Cloughton	35	Harpooner	Gateshead
Thomas Ditchburn	20	Harpooner	Shields
Thomas Atkins	28	Harpooner	Shields
William Atkins	28	Harpooner	Shields
William Harcull	30	Seaman	Shields
James Jeffels	29	Seaman	Shields
George Smith	34	Seaman	Yorkshire/Shields
John Harland	27	Seaman	Blyth
John Whillock	25	Seaman	Newcastle
William Harrison	30	Seaman	Newcastle
Robert Richardson	45	Seaman	Newcastle
James Brownie	21	Seaman	Shields
James Burkill	26	Seaman	Shields
Joseph Hutchinson	20	Seaman	Shields
Philip Ferguson	26	Seaman	Newcastle
James Nicholson		Seaman	Newcastle
John Jackson	37	Seaman	Newcastle
Thomas Hutchinson	30	Cooper	Shields
Alex Castles	29	Seaman	Shields
John Smith	21	Carpenter	Ireland/Shields
Andrew Maddison	20	Carpenter	Shields
John Coble	38	Seaman	Newcastle
Gilbert Mackenzie	21	Seaman	Shields
Mathew Hall	23	Seaman	Shields
Joseph Fourine	32	Seaman	Newcastle
Robert Silcock	18	Seaman	Newcastle
George Gibson	14	Seaman	Newcastle
Edward Park	15	Seaman	Newcastle
George Irvin	14	Seaman	Newcastle

(continued)

Kitty, 1783

Port: Shields

Name	*Age*	*Position*	*Where Born/Abode*
William Thirdson	19	Seaman	Newcastle
James Bird	18	Seaman	Durham/Shields
Henry Wishart	20	Seaman	Newcastle
Andrew Finlayson	14	Seaman	Newcastle
Joseph Mackay	19	Seaman	Hexham/Shields
George Law	16	Seaman	Scotland/Shetland
Andrew North	15	Seaman	Scotland/Shetland
Robert Herron	13	Seaman	Scotland/Shetland
Peter Leask	15	Seaman	Scotland/Shetland

Source: PRO, BT 98/131 No. 209

Sarah, 1784

Port: Shields

Name	*Age*	*Position*	*Where Born/Abode*
Thomas Frank, Jnr.	35	Master	Newcastle/Newcastle
Bartholomew Robson	35	First mate	Newcastle/Newcastle
Robert Burley	49	Carpenter	Newcastle/Newcastle
John Curry	49	Carpenter's mate	Shields/Newcastle
Thomas Trotter	25	Boatswain	Shields/Newcastle
Richard Day	37	Harpooner	Lynn/Newcastle
Samuel Dodds	45	Cooper	Newcastle/Newcastle
William Ramsay	20	Cook's mate	Swalwell/Newcastle
Abraham Barpie	40	Cook	Leith/Newcastle
Luke Kirk	30	Harpooner	Lynn/Lynn
Max Hopper	28	Boatsteerer	Shields/Shields
James Metcalfe	30	Boatsteerer	Shields/Shields
William Anderson	26	Boatsteerer	Whitby/Whitby
Ralph Thompson	30	Boatsteerer	Blyth/Blyth
Robert Ward	23	Boatsteerer	Whitby/Whitby
John Anderson	29	Boatsteerer	Whitby/Whitby
Andrew Spence	22	Line manager	Orkney/Shields
John Church	21	Line manager	Harwich/Harwich
Edward Morris	27	Line manager	Shetland/Shields
Christopher Willson	26	Line manager	Sunderland/Sunderland
George Shields	30	Line manager	Cockermouth/Shields
Robert Simons	30	Seaman	Newcastle/Newcastle
John Watson	27	Seaman	Newcastle/Newcastle
John Bayne	20	Seaman	Leith/Newcastle
Abraham Brady	22	Seaman	Leith/Newcastle
Jacob Urwin	50	Seaman	Shields/Shields
Leo Cunningham	40	Seaman	Newcastle/Newcastle
William Owen	30	Seaman	Orkney/Orkney
Robert Scotland	20	Seaman	Orkney/Orkney
Magnus Sinclair	30	Seaman	Orkney/Orkney
William Allans	32	Seaman	Orkney/Orkney
Hubert Dorrison	20	Seaman	Orkney/Orkney
Thomas Dorrison	20	Seaman	Orkney/Shields

Source: PRO, BT 98/132, No. 113

Disko Bay, 1788

Port: Shields

Name	*Age*	*Position*	*Where Born/Abode*
William Hamilton	44	Master	Newcastle
Pat Craigie	19	Surgeon	Perth
George Harrison	25	First mate	Newcastle
John Cave	26	Spectioneer	Newcastle
William Sutcliffe	23	Harpooner	Newcastle
Hazell Legg	33	Second mate	North Shields
Alex Cummins	40	Harpooner	North Shields
Henry Nisbett	24	Carpenter	North Shields
William Muckle	29	Boatsteerer	Newcastle
Robert Black	23	Boatsteerer	Newcastle
James Hallinam	20	Boatsteerer	Newcastle
Stephen Millner	29	Boatsteerer	Newcastle
Alex Williamson	31	Line manager	Newcastle
Francis Greatman	20	Line manager	North Shields
David Quivrie	28	Line manager	Newcastle
William Price	24	Line manager	Newcastle
William Martin	31	Line manager	Newcastle
Joseph Spottswood	26	Line manager	Newcastle
Reginald Robson	20	Cooper	Newcastle
James Taylor	28	Cooper's mate	Newcastle
Joseph Willson	23	Carpenter's mate	Newcastle
George George	26	Landsman	Newcastle
Francis Dobinson	23	Landsman	Heworth
Jacob Davidson	20	Seaman	Heworth
William Higgs	21	Seaman	Newcastle
Marcus Bell	40	Cook	North Shields
John Maine	25	Seaman	North Shields
Peter Newcater	20	Seaman	North Shields
Robert Briscoe	30	Seaman	Whitehaven
James Corner	19	Seaman	Newcastle
James Ross	20	Seaman	Newcastle
John Richardson	20	Seaman	Newcastle
Matthew Ritchie	22	Seaman	Newcastle
John Isbister	21	Seaman	Newcastle
Joseph Gladstone	21	Seaman	Newcastle
Magnus Kirkup	21	Seaman	Newcastle
John Sindcup	21	Seaman	Newcastle

Source: PRO, BT 98/132, No. 92

Phoenix, 1836

Port: Whitby

Name	*Age*	*Position*	*Where Born/Abode*
Thomas Mills	48	Master	North Shields
Robert Wyllie	21	Surgeon	Montrose
William Stead	28	Mate & harpooner	Middleton
William May	34	Second mate & harpooner	Prestonpans
John Welch	41	Spectioneer & harpooner	Cockenzie
Thomas Jenkinson	44	Harpooner	Loftus
Adam Stainsby	38	Loose harpooner	Stockton
William Sleightholme	33	Loose harpooner	Whitby
Lawrence Gehan	35	Boatsteerer	Easington
David Robinson	41	Boatsteerer	Whitby
John Harrison	44	Boatsteerer	Stainsacre
Robert Holdsforth	35	Boatsteerer	Ruswarp
Edward Bedlington Jnr.	24	Boatsteerer	Robin Hood's Bay
Francis Nossiter	33	Boatsteerer	Whitby
Robert Jackson	29	Line manager	Whitby
Timothy Duck	-	Line manager	Whitby
Harrison Rippon	18	Line manager	Whitby
Mark Dring	39	Carpenter	Whitby
Ralph Hodgson	21	Carpenter's mate	Whitby
John Hopes	42	Cooper	Penrith
Edward Bedlington Snr.	60	Cook	Robin Hood's Bay
Francis Lorains	26	Cook's mate	Whitby
John Elliot Lund	15	Apprentice	Whitby
James Hartley	-	Apprentice	Whitby
William Gibson	12	Apprentice	Whitby
Magnus Houston	23	Seaman	Harray
James Backie	24	Seaman	Harray
John Backie	19	Seaman	Harray
James Harper	25	Seaman	Stromness
John Linklater	36	Seaman	Birsay
John Rowland	20	Seaman	Stromness
James Backie Jnr.	17	Seaman	Stromness
William Brass	26	Seaman	Sandwick
John Merriman	23	Seaman	Harray
William Backie	21	Seaman	Harray

(continued)

Phoenix, 1836

Port: Whitby

Name	*Age*	*Position*	*Where Born/Abode*
James Leask	26	Seaman	Stromness
William Leask	24	Seaman	Stromness
William Spence	30	Seaman	Stromness
Peter Johnston	25	Seaman	Stromness
Donald Thompson	19	Seaman	South Ronaldsay
Magnus Smith	19	Seaman	Harray
Magnus Mowat	20	Seaman	Island of Graemsay
John Twatt	27	Seaman	Harray
Alexander Harvey	21	Seaman	Sandwick
Thomas Taylor	22	Seaman	Birsay
George Sinclair	22	Seaman	Graemsay
Charles Ritch	20	Seaman	Graemsay
Thomas Bell	21	Seaman	Stromness
James Rowland	21	Seaman	Birsay
John Johnston	20	Seaman	Birsay

Source: PRO, BT 98/523,

Camden, 1836

Port: Whitby

Name	*Age*	*Position*	*Where Born/Abode*
(16 March - 25 October)			
John Armstrong	46	Master	Cullercoats
Thomas Johnson	19	Surgeon	Biggar
John Patterson	33	Mate/Hpr.	North Shields
George Winlow	36	Second mate	Newton
William Wilson	47	Spec./Hpr.	North Shields
Thomas Gibson	25	Bosun	Whitby
Thomas Robson	35	Harpooner	Newburn
William Hume	31	Loose	North Shields
Thomas Pearson	40	Boatsteerer	Whitby
Richard Purvis	26	Boatsteerer	Whitby
William Andrew	29	Boatsteerer	Whitby
James Shipley	28	Boatsteerer	North Shields
Roger Hall	27	Boatsteerer	North Shields
David Nairn	28	Boatsteerer	Stromness
William Mills	25	Line manager	North Shields
Frank Pattison	21	Line manager	Whitby
William Langhorn	23	Line manager	Whitby
Thomas Corner	24	Line manager	Whitby
John Raistrick	48	Carpenter	Whitby
William Alderson	21	Carpenter's mate	Egton
William Carter	28	Cooper	Lythe
James Ward	44	Cook	Whitby
William Moorson	51	Cook's mate	Robin Hood's Bay
William Dawson Mills	19	Apprentice	London
John Pevotam	17	Apprentice	-
George Brown	16	Apprentice	Easingwold
William Gatenby	14	Apprentice	Whitby

(continued)

Camden, 1836

Port: Whitby

Name	*Age*	*Position*	*Where Born/Abode*
At Stromness (25 March - 23 October)			
John Leask	22	Seaman	Stenness
John Corrigall	23	Seaman	Sandwick
Nicol Duskson	25	Seaman	Stenness
Peter Tait	33	Seaman	Stenness
John Houston	29	Seaman	Harra
Andrew Dickson	27	Seaman	Stenness
William Clouston	25	Seaman	Stenness
Harry Garrioch	28	Seaman	Ireland
Thomas Slettar	20	Seaman	Stenness
George Moor	27	Seaman	Sandwick
Hugh Knarston	29	Seaman	Hoy
Thomas Ritch	30	Seaman	Graemsay
John Sutherland	21	Seaman	Hoy
James McKenzie	22	Seaman	Hoy
James Mellior	20	Seaman	S. Ronaldsay
George Flett	25	Seaman	Orphir
John Garson	21	Seaman	Sandwick
John Paplay	19	Seaman	Stenness
David Brass	19	Seaman	Sandwick
Charles Ritch	21	Seaman	Graemsay
Henry Wilson	23	Seaman	Graemsay
James Linklator	19	Seaman	Stenness
James Thompson	23	Seaman	Graemsay
Magnus Linklator	26	Seaman	Birsay

Source: PRO BT 98/519

Norfolk, 1836

Port: Berwick

Name	*Age*	*Position*	*Where Born/Abode*	*Remarks*
George Harrison	40	Master	Hartley	
James Ford	25	Surgeon	Edinburgh	
Robert Laidler	43	Mate	Murton Sq	
John Irvine Curry	34	Second mate	Leith	
Thomas Hall	47	Harpooner	Tweedmouth	Died 23 March 1837
Peter Horn	43	Harpooner	Cockenzie	
Angus McKenzie	34	Bosun	Prestonpans	
James Johnson	30	Harpooner	Cockenzie	
James Ritchie	29	Harpooner	Cockenzie	
John Douglas	38	Carpenter	Berwick	
Michael Knox	34	Boatsteerer	Berwick	
George Jackson	30	Boatsteerer	Spittal	
William Jackson	22	Boatsteerer	Spittal	
John Laidler	24	Boatsteerer	East Ord	
William Cockburn	24	Boatsteerer	Spittal	
George Leith	41	Sailmaker	Berwick	Died 17 March 1837
Alexander Allen	25	Line manager	Tweedmouth	
George Dixon	29	Line manager	Spittal	
Peter Knox	23	Line manager	Ancroft	
Thomas Lilly	25	Line manager	East Ord	Died 15 March 1837
Thomas Todd	26	Line manager	Spittal	
Thomas Yetman	31	Line manager	Bristol	Died 14 March 1837
John Middleton	23	Line manager	Berwick	
Thomas Crowther	37	Cooper	Tweedmouth	
George Hastie	29	Cooper's mate	Tweedmouth	
James Dixon	57	Cook	Berwick	Died 22 March 1837
James How	29	Seaman	Berwick	
John Swan	18	Apprentice	Berwick	
William Gray	19	Apprentice	Spittal	
Andrew Gray	17	Apprentice	Spittal	
John Swiney	20	Apprentice	Spittal	

31 men mustered to *Norfolk* of Berwick on 14 April 1836, of whom 5 died and were buried at sea, a further 19 seamen were taken on board at Stromness, of whom 5 died at sea on 8 and 9 February, 1 March, 15 March and 30 March 1837. *Norfolk* also took 13 seamen from *Thomas* of Dundee, wrecked in the ice on 16 December 1836. Of these, 8 died on 8 February, 12, 15, 17, 24, 26, 27 and 28 March.

Source: PRO, BT 98/174.

Lady Jane, 1838

Port: Shields

Name	*Age*	*Position*	*Where Born/ Abode*	*Remarks*
George Harrison	42	Master	Hartley	
John Patterson	36	First mate	North Shields	
Robert Thompson	39	Second mate	Prestonpans	
George Winlow	40	Seaman	Newton	
Thomas Thompson	39	Seaman	Prestonpans	
Thomas Jameson	21	Surgeon	South Shields	Buried Davis Straits
Andrew Stewart	40	Seaman	Cockenzie	
Robert Duncan	28	Seaman	Cullercoats	
Alexander Coult	37	Seaman	Prestonpans	
Robert Stewart	23	Seaman	Cockenzie	
Alexander Thompson	36	Seaman	Prestonpans	
David Ross	25	Seaman	Cockenzie	
Richard Livingstone	26	Seaman	Prestonpans	
Donald McBane	29	Seaman	North Shields	
George Hope	39	Carpenter	South Shields	
William Boston	36	Cooper	Spittal	
Lowery Moat	43	Seaman	Shetland	
Thomas Mackay	21	Seaman	Prestonpans	
Robert Rochester	25	Sailmaker	Newcastle	
Robert Stewart	48	Seaman	St.Christophorus	
William Hanney	25	Seaman	Hull	
Ralph Reid	22	Carpenter's mate	Newcastle	
William Grey	21	Cooper's mate	Hibblesworth	
Luke Wilkinson	41	Cook	Tynemouth	
John Taylor	13	Boy	Cullercoats	
John Batsford	23	Seaman	Stebbing	
Henry Bowes	28	Seaman	Hull	
Robert Johnston	41	Seaman	Birsay	
James Holland	44	Seaman	Frith	
William Corston	22	Seaman		
William Haroy	25	Seaman	Birsay	
James Moar	27	Seaman	Birsay	
George Stranger	19	Seaman	Birsay	
James Murray	22	Seaman	Houton	

(continued)

Lady Jane, 1838

Port: Shields

Name	*Age*	*Position*	*Where Born/Abode*	*Remarks*
William Clouston	30	Seaman		
- Kirkpatrick	20	Seaman		
Robert Linney	40	Seaman	Stromness	
Andrew Garson	32	Seaman	Birsay	
James Clouston	23	Seaman	Stromness	
John Garson	24	Seaman	Sandwick	
Magnus Linklater	31	Seaman	Birsay	
John Taylor	31	Seaman	Birsay	
Peter Murray	24	Seaman	Orpher	
Thomas Hewiston	27	Seaman	Harray	
David White	33	Seaman	Stromness	
John Johnston	43	Seaman	Sandwick	
James Irvine	24	Seaman	Rendall	
Isaac Johnston	39	Seaman		
John Linklater	50	Seaman	Birsay	
Edward Irvine	22	Seaman	Stromness	
James Mowat	18	Apprentice	Spittal	
Robert McDougal	20	Apprentice	Spittal	

Source: PRO BT 98/420.

Grenville Bay, 1840

Port: Shields

Name	*Age*	*Position*	*Where Born/Abode*
Thomas Taylor	42	Master	North Shields
William Newbould	50	Mate	North Shields
William Wilson	47	Spectioneer	North Shields
Peter Murray	39	Boatsteerer	Prestonpans
William Thompson	36	Second mate	Prestonpans
George Edmond	52	Harpooner	Prestonpans
Robert Patterson	44	Harpooner	Prestonpans
James Binthouse	29	Harpooner	Inchbeck
Thomas Sutherland	31	Boatsteerer	North Shields
Alex Sutton	31	Boatsteerer	Fisherow
James Anderson	21	Boatsteerer	Prestonpans
Alex Dicky	23	Seaman	North Shields
James Thompson	21	Seaman	North Shields
William Knight	19	Seaman	Thornham
John Weatherstone	19	Cook	Newcastle
John Carr	29	Steward	Brock Mill
John Hopper	34	Carpenter	South Shields
John Johnson	32	Cooper	Spittal
Robert Carruthers	21	Sailmaker	South Shields
- Ormond	21	Cooper's mate	Alnwick
Joseph Stewart	21	Seaman	North Shields
Alex Thompson	28	Boatsteerer	North Shields
Lawrence Ramsey	24	Seaman	Shetland
John Brown	24	Seaman	Yarmouth
John Henry	40	Seaman	Bluncastle
Walter Davison	43	Seaman	Shetland
Henry Grice	22	Seaman	Yarmouth
Joseph Gray	35	Boatsteerer	North Shields
Robert Baker	21	Seaman	North Shields
John Newby	21	Seaman	North Shields
William Oakley	27	Boatsteerer	Prestonpans

Another 19 seamen mustered at Stromness

Source: PRO, BT 98/416.

Lord Gambier, 1841

Port: Shields

Name	*Age*	*Born*	*Position*
Richard Warham	45	Leeds	Master
James Ferguson	20	Edinburgh	Surgeon
John Wheatley	53	Felling	Mate
Jonathon Markham	32	North Shields	Second mate
John Welsh	51	Cockenzie	Spectioneer
George Fair	31	North Shields	Harpooner
William Spence	41	Stromness	Harpooner
William Horn	33		Harpooner
John Hardwick	36	Jarrow	Harpooner
John Hopper	34	South Shields	Carpenter
John Fitchard	62	Bridgetown	Cook
Adam Robertson	42	Tweedmouth	Cooper
George Smith	27	North Shields	Harpooner
John Ritch	36	Graemsay	Boatsteerer
Magnus Johnston	27	Birsay	Boatsteerer
James Forster	26	Graemsay	Boatsteerer
John Christie	27	North Shields	Sailmaker
Thomas Nicholson	21	Newcastle	Steward
Joseph Dixon	27	North Shields	Boatsteerer
James Young	25	Inverkeithy	Boatsteerer
Ralph Dawson	20	North Shields	Seaman
Richard Ross	20	Edinburgh	Seaman
Joseph Johnson	33	Spittal	Cooper's mate
Robert Archibald	20	Stromness	Seaman
James Albey	24	South Shields	Seaman
Robert Jenkins	22	North Shields	Seaman
Joseph Lamb	24	North Shields	Carpenter's mate
Alex Dykes	24	North Shields	Seaman
John Randy	21	North Shields	Seaman
Robert Bruce	33	North Shields	Seaman
James Brown	26	Newcastle	Cook's mate
Thomas Rigby	12	North Shields	Boy

Another 18 seamen mustered at Stromness.

Source: PRO, BT 98/416.

Lady Jane, 1848

Port: Shields

Name	*Age*	*Position*	*Where Born/Abode*
John Patterson	48	Master	North Shields
William Archibald	42	Mate	Path Head
Donald McLeod	21	Surgeon/Harpooner	Glenmoriston
Robert Thompson	44	Second mate/Harpooner	Prestonpans
William Thompson	44	Spectioneer	Prestonpans
Alex Thompson	34	Harpooner	Prestonpans
Robert McDougle	27	Loose harpooner	Spittal
William Colston	30	Loose harpooner	Cockenzie
George Winlow	49	Harpooner/Boatswain	Newton
James Watson	48	Boatsteerer	Kirkaldy
Alex Coll	46	Boatsteerer	Prestonpans
Alex Horn	26	Boatsteerer	Cockenzie
James Stewart	24	Boatsteerer	Cockenzie
Alex Thompson	22	Boatsteerer	Prestonpans
Thomas Mackie	27	Boatsteerer	Prestonpans
William Boston	44	Cooper	Spittal
Edward Doundsy	44	Carpenter	South Shields
John White	29	Sailmaker	South Shields
James Lamb	30	Carpenter's mate	Percy Main
Joseph Johnson	40	Cooper's mate	Spittal
John Weatherston	40	Cook	Newcastle
George Patterson	22	Line coiler	South Shields
William B. Taylor	19	Line coiler	Berwick
Lawrence Moat	45	Cook's mate	Lerwick
John Cockburn	25	Line coiler	South Shields
Anthony Mayer	21	Line coiler	South Shields
Adam Horn	19	Line coiler	Cockenzie
William Rigby	24	Line coiler	South Shields
John Reed	25	Line coiler	Berwick
William Miller	48	Line coiler	Balty Sound
William Harrison	17	Apprentice	North Shields

17 seamen, 1 blacksmith, 1 steward and 2 apprentices joined at Stromness

Source: PRO, BT 98/1709

Select bibliography

The maritime history of north-east England remains a remarkably under-researched and under-published field of regional history, despite the wealth of historical evidence available to sustain it. The following select bibliography offers some suggested additional reading for those who might wish to pursue their interests a little further.

Adlard, M. *The Greenlander*, Penguin Books, Harmondsworth, 1980.
A well-researched and written novel of Whitby whaling by a local author. The book represents an excellent introduction to the topic for the general reader.

Barron, W. *Old Whaling Days*, Conway Maritime Press, London, 1970.
A reprint of a book first published in 1895. One of the classic, first-hand accounts of whaling under sail in the mid-nineteenth century. Barron first sailed to the Arctic as an apprentice on *Truelove* of Hull in 1849 and rose to command whale ships from that port in the 1860s.

Barrow, T. (ed.) *Press Gangs and Privateers*, Bewick Press, Whitley Bay, 1993.
A brief 'Collected Essays' volume which includes an account of the *Noble Ann Affair*, when angry Greenlanders clashed with the press gang at the mouth of the Tyne in 1779.

Francis, D. *Arctic Chase*, Breakwater Books, St. John's, Newfoundland, 1984.
A popular account of whaling in the Canadian Arctic and a good general introduction to the subject.

Gaskell, E. *Sylvia's Lovers*, Oxford Paperbacks, Oxford, 1999.
Gaskell's novel is set in Whitby and the hero a harpooner aboard a local ship. The story provides an accurate, if rather romantic, account of press gangs and whalermen.

Gillies-Ross, W. *Arctic Whalers, Icy Seas: Narratives of Davis Straits Whaling, 1824-1917*, Irwin Publishing, Toronto, 1985.

A collection of eye-witness accounts written principally by officers and surgeons of British whalers, including narratives of experiences during the notorious 1835-36 and 1836-37 seasons.

Jackson, G. *The British Whaling Trade*, Adam and Charles Black, London, 1978.

Remains the best academic account of the rise and fall of British whaling enterprise. A 'must read' for anyone concerned to develop their knowledge of this branch of the trade.

Keys, R.E. *A Dictionary of Tyne Sailing Ships, 1830-1930*, R.E. Keys, Newcastle, 1998.

A comprehensive work of reference for students of regional shipping and the shipping industry during the nineteenth century. Includes summaries of the various trades in which Tyneside ships were engaged as well as ownership details and vessel histories.

Lubbock, B. *The Arctic Whalers*, Brown Son and Ferguson, Glasgow, 1937.

A basic source for students of the Northern Whale Fishery but is more concerned with the ships and men than with the economics of the whaling trade. Frustratingly under-referenced and occasionally inaccurate.

Osler, A. and Barrow, A. *Tall Ships: Two Rivers*, Keepdate, Newcastle, 1993.

Represents the only modern, general account of the shipping and trade of the Tyne and Wear in the age of sail. A standard reference book for many aspects of 'Maritime Northumbria'.

Scoresby, W. *An Account of the Arctic Regions with a History and Description of the Northern Whale Fishery*, (2 volumes), Constable, Edinburgh, 1820.

Volume 2 remains a standard work on the Greenland Whale Fishery. Also contains a rare contemporary description of the structures, equipment and processes of whale oil manufacture.

Stamp, T & C. *Greenland Voyager*, Caedmon of Whitby, 1983.

A compilation of entries from Scoresby's logbooks and journals contained within the Scoresby Archive of Whitby Literary and Philosophical Society. Provides an excellent insight into the everyday business of Whitby whaling.

Stamp, T & C. *William Scoresby, Arctic Scientist*, Caedmon of Whitby, 1976.
The only biography of a North East whaler captain, concentrating on the scientific observations and experiments of Whitby's most celebrated whaling son.

Troup, J.A. (ed.) *The Icebound Whalers*, The Orkney Press, Stromness, 1987.
Two eye-witness accounts drawn from the diaries of Orkneymen who served aboard *Dee* of Aberdeen and *Grenville Bay* of Newcastle during the ice-drift voyages of 1836-37. The editor is an expert on Orkney and Arctic whaling and supports the narratives with detailed contextual information.

Index

Merchants and Gentry in North-East England 1650-1830
The Carrs and the Ellisons

This book follows the progress of the Ellisons of Hebburn Hall and the Carrs of Dunston Hill from their mercantile success in the seventeenth century to their solid gentry and land-owning status in the nineteenth century.

The aim of this book is to set the history of the Carrs and Ellisons against the development of the region on which they made such an influence, thus uncovering such issues as:

social mobility - economic advancement - money and health - political power - patronage - manners and mores - marriage as a means of economic and social advancement - relationship between land and commerce.

The main source of research is drawn from the wealth of papers collected by both families providing considerable information about social and family lives of the North East elite during the period 1650-1830. Particular emphasis is placed upon the question of social mobility and upon relations between merchants and gentry.

The Millennium History of North East England

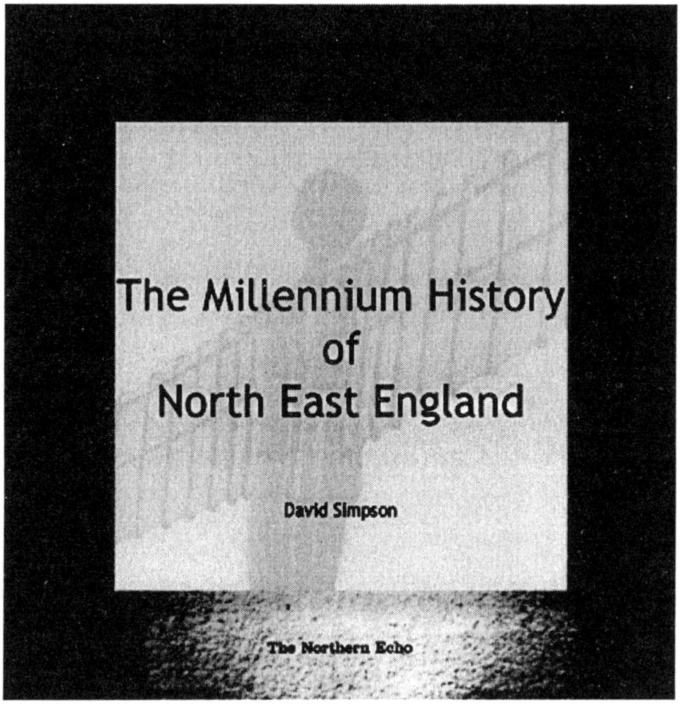

North East England has a strong sense of identity that sets it apart from other areas of England. The roots of this identity lie in two thousand years of distinct history that have made the region what it is today.

From the Roman frontier zone of Hadrian's Wall, to the powerful Christian Kingdom of Northumbria, through the gloomy days of Border warfare up to the great age of coal mining and railways, each era has played its part.

This unique, 336 page beautifully illustrated hardback book explores the events, people and places that have shaped the region's history over the last two thousand years.

To order contact: Business Education Publishers Ltd.,
The Solar Building, Doxford International,
Sunderland, SR3 3XW.
Tel: +44(0)191 525 2410   Fax: +44(0)191 520 1815   email: sales@bepl.com
Retail price: £19.99 plus postage on single orders
ISBN No. 0-9536984-3-2

The Millennium History of North East England